THE
WAY
OF THE
WILL

THE
WAY
OF THE
WILL

Thelema in Action

DAVID SHOEMAKER

WEISER BOOKS

This edition first published in 2024 by Weiser Books, an imprint of
Red Wheel/Weiser, LLC

With offices at:
65 Parker Street, Suite 7
Newburyport, MA 01950
www.redwheelweiser.com

ISBN: 978-1-57863-826-0
Library of Congress Cataloging-in-Publication Data available upon request.

Cover design by Sky Peck Design
Interior by Maureen Forys, Happenstance Type-O-Rama
Typeset in Garamond Premier Pro, Montserrat, and Shango

Figures 3–6: Thomas Nelson Stewart IV
The Living Thelema name and all associated content © David Shoemaker
Phyllis Seckler material © Temple of the Silver Star
Transcription by Kelli Patton

Printed in the United States of America
IBI

10 9 8 7 6 5 4 3 2 1

A∴A∴

Publication in Class B

Imprimatur:

93	10°=1□	**PRO COLL. SUMM.**
666	9°=2□	
V.V.V.V.V.	8°=3□	
Σ	8°=3□	
I.	7°=4□	**PRO COLL. INT.**
V.V.	6°=5□	
L.	5°=6□	
I.	Praem.	**PRO COLL. EXT.**
A.S.B.	Imp.	
L.L.L.	Canc.	

Unto Thee, my Lord Σ.......,
This kiss,
This soul,
This heart!

Thou shalt mingle thy life with the universal life.

—LIBER CHETH VEL VALLUM ABIEGNI

TABLE OF CONTENTS

ACKNOWLEDGMENTS

I offer my eternal gratitude to my teachers across time and distance, Aleister Crowley, Karl Germer, Jane Wolfe, and Phyllis Seckler, without whom the Great Work of Thelema would not exist as we know it. Many thanks also to Lon Milo DuQuette, Richard Kaczynski, Robert Fripp, David Singleton, my students, clients, family, friends, and magical colleagues, and my wonderful wife Lauren, for their support and wisdom over the years.

INTRODUCTION

Do what thou wilt shall be the whole of the Law.

The world has changed. The Great Work of self-transformation, in all its fundamntals, has not.

Since the original publication of my book *Living Thelema* in 2013, the world has experienced incredible changes in its politics, climate, technology, social and cultural conditions, and seemingly every other area one might consider. Sometimes I hardly recognize my own life from a decade ago, and I'm sure you, the reader, can relate. What do we do when the familiar, the comfortable, the safe, the reliable is snatched away and replaced by uncertainty, and the disorientation and fear that often accompany it? What is left of us when those outer husks of stability and identity are stripped away?

If this question is relevant for this last decade of humanity's existence, it is surely even more so when considering our evolution as a species over the last several millennia. To my own question above, *What is left of us?* when all this change is afoot, I answer: Only what is *essential* to our survival. At the core of every human is something immutable and immortal. Something which is so truly essential to our being that we would not be fully human without it. This star at the center of our own personal solar system is the real spiritual source of our selfhood, and cultivating a vibrant, conscious link between it and our everyday personality is one way of describing what we call the Great Work.

In the tradition of Thelema, many of us believe that our connection to this central star-self is the key to understanding the True Will, the basic nature of our existence—the unique "formula" each of us instinctively employs as we navigate the inner and outer world. Discovering this True Will with full consciousness and clarity, and then living it out with efficiency, passion, and joy, is the lifeline we all need in a world filled with constant change. *This* is what is essential to our survival—this Great Work of personal transformation—and the theory and practice of Thelema offer many keys.

AN OVERVIEW OF THE BOOK

In *Living Thelema,* I covered many of the basic principles and practices of Thelema, as well as more advanced concepts. If you have not yet done so, I encourage you to review its contents alongside the material here. My aim with the present volume is to elaborate on the ways in which Aleister Crowley's Thelema can be utilized to enhance your experience of the world, as well as your psychological and spiritual growth. Along the way, I will present my own musings on the role of key Thelemic practices in this work, often based on material originally presented by Crowley in his instructional *libers.* These chapters grew out of a diversity of my own teachings and experiences—podcast episodes, classes, and of course, many years of personal practice and supervision of other initiates. Accordingly, this volume does not serve as a comprehensive review or summary of Thelemic theory and practice; rather, it is a compendium of tools and perspectives designed to serve as *one* of many useful tomes in the magician's library.

In Part One of the book, *Qabalah, the Path of Initiation, and the Life Within,* we'll look at ways your inner experience can be enhanced by tools such as the Qabalistic Tree of Life, Qabalistic psychology, and the symbolic world of astrology. We'll also review the ways in which Thelema can inform your creativity, your sense of connectedness and meaning, and your experience of the nature of life itself. Finally, we'll discuss the inevitable ordeals that impact us along the path of the Great Work, and ways to cope with them.

In Part Two, *Thelemic Practice in Detail,* we'll review several important (but rarely discussed) advanced meditation practices in the Thelemic corpus, with an eye toward strengthening your use of these powerful practices with no-nonsense advice. I'll give tips for constructing powerful, customized magical[1] invocations. Then we'll examine the deeper, personal magick accessible via attendance of the *Gnostic Mass*, and the ways the core landmarks of the original Hermetic Order of the Golden Dawn can be (and have been) adapted to express and enhance Thelemic principles and practices. Finally, I will offer a personal memoir of my own path toward awareness of True Will, including my experience of the "Knowledge and Conversation of the Holy Guardian Angel"—the term used by Crowley to describe the pivotal spiritual awakening potentially available to every human being.

∴

What is essential to *your* survival? To *your* basic nature? To *your* transcendence of the limitations of the everyday human personality and its strivings? Only you can answer these questions, of course, but it is my hope that the present volume may provide useful and powerful tools for your journey.

Love is the law, love under will.

—DAVID SHOEMAKER
RALEIGH, North Carolina
SPRING EQUINOX 2023 E.V.

---

[1] Note my spelling of the word *magical,* without the *k,* which matches Crowley's usage. He added the *k* when spelling the root word *magick,* but not in his spelling of related terms such as *magical* or *magician.* (This footnote was brought to you by the Virgo placement of the sun and many other planets in my natal horoscope. I continue to await patiently the compliance of the entire magical community.)

PART ONE

Qabalah, the Path of Initiation,
and the Life Within

CHAPTER 1

ADVICE FROM
THE TREE OF LIFE

As has often been said, the Qabalistic Tree of Life is a complete map of the human self, in all its fullness. Rightly understood, it encompasses every region of human consciousness, and every conceivable change process available to that consciousness. It should not be surprising, then, that we can turn to this resource for aid in the many troublesome situations that arise in life. In this chapter, we'll review the nature of the sephiroth on the Tree, and explore the "advice" available to us when we encounter those inevitable stuck places, obstacles, and points of confusion. The process is nuanced, but not unduly complex. Essentially, we tune in to our understanding of what each of the sephiroth embodies in its full and healthful expression, as well as its *qlippothic* or "shadow" side. We then check in with ourselves, and assess how we are doing in carrying out the overall task of *embodying* the Tree. Are we balanced, or are we overemphasizing a particular aspect of self? If we are unbalanced, how do we correct or compensate for that? We'll begin by reviewing each sephira in turn, starting with Malkuth and working our way up the Tree. After completing our journey to Kether, we'll discuss some practical tips for applying these principles.

When evaluating the shadow side of these regions of self, it is interesting to note that this is not so much about an absence of the sephira's characteristics, but rather an excessive or misguided application of them. It's important to make this distinction, because this is not a simplistic assessment that shadow-stuff is "bad," and the absence of it is "good." Rather, it is by seeking out and acknowledging our shadow material that we are pointed to avenues of healing and growth. When we identify a problem pattern and can locate it on the Tree, we are given clues about how we might transmute it into the positive expression of the *same energy*. In doing this, we are literally "redeeming" the *qlippoth* by putting them in constructive service to the sephira. The key questions are along the lines of: What would the sephira *want* me to do to express and fulfill its inherent nature? What advice would it therefore give me in order to deal with the problem I'm facing? For each of the sephiroth below, it should be fairly self-evident how we might steer ourselves from the shadow side back to a balanced and healthful expression of the essential nature of the sephira in question. Much of the time, gaining awareness of the problematic pattern, and setting the intention to connect with the healthful side, is itself sufficient to get some positive momentum.

Malkuth, in its fullness, is the domain of physical health, pleasurable immersion in the world of sensation, practicality, and finding the divine in all of physical manifestation. The shadow side of Malkuth includes overindulgence, laziness, excessive pleasure-focus at the expense of constructive self-discipline, distraction from spiritual aims due to absorption in practicalities, and similar pitfalls.

Yesod, in its fullness, encompasses vitality, virility, fertility, and an unblocked flow of energy. Unconscious contents of the mind are not unduly repressed; that is, the conscious and unconscious function unhindered and cooperatively, and there is substantial conscious awareness of potential unconscious patterns. The shadow expression of Yesod includes sexual obsession or aggression, creative sterility, an absence of sexual interest (if otherwise desired), excessive projection of repressed or ignored

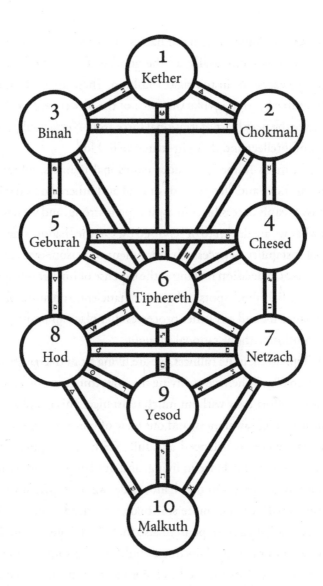

unconscious contents, mismanagement of the life force, energetic deple-
tion, and undue dependence on people or substances.

With Hod, in its fullness, we see intellectual acuity, the easy flow of
ideas, accurate self-analysis, good organizational skills and task execution, and ease with verbal and written expression of ideas. The shadow
side includes overly rigid thought structures, abandonment of feeling

in service to cold logic, clinging to habits or structures in our daily lives without flexibility—essentially, all the good stuff that the intellect can do is done to excess, or in too rigid a fashion. These are indeed the sorts of rigidities that tend to invoke the force of the Tower card of the Tarot, where we see the fiery blast of irrational force from Netzach blasting apart the tower of intellect and thought structure in Hod.

Netzach, in its fullness, includes emotional richness, vibrancy, and engagement. Love and affection for oneself and others flows freely, spiritual ecstasy is easily accessible, our aspiration is strong, and we have a clear sense of what we are drawn to or repulsed by. On the shadow side, we have emotional instability or excess, abandonment of reason, overreliance on likes or dislikes in decision making at the expense of further self-reflection on our potential blind spots, religious fanaticism, romantic obsessions that unbalance us, and any other processes that place an undue emphasis on pure emotion without rational thought.

With Tiphareth, in its fullness, we are living from the spiritual center of our personality. When we are living this way, things in our lives tend to "click" rather effortlessly without much resistance. This is a place of spiritually informed self-awareness, and our view of our own ego/personality structure as a whole is balanced and full. We have an appreciation for beauty, harmony, and balance in living, and our cooperation with others is harmonious and easy. On the shadow side, we see spiritual vanity and spiritual materialism: "I'm more spiritually advanced than you, so I am better than you." Shadow-Tiphareth also includes the guru complex, and overlooking our practical affairs due to unhealthy absorption in spiritual matters. At some points we need to focus more on spiritual matters, but at others we really do need to tighten up the nuts and bolts of our lives in a practical sense!

Geburah, in its fullness, brings energetic action, a life lived in accordance with True Will, decisive application of the proper force to the proper ends in our actions, enacting justice, and living without fear. On the shadow side, not unexpectedly, we see undue aggression or tyranny, failure to honor the rights of others in the pursuit of our own ends, and blind force carelessly applied. This is essentially a "shotgun" approach to life, when our courage has turned into foolhardiness, or our strength into mere cruelty and efforts at domination.

With Chesed, in its fullness, we are living from a place of spiritual awareness and balanced leadership. This may be social leadership, but it is also importantly a regulation of our own *ruach* via full self-awareness and linkage to the higher self. We have a loving and solemn responsibility for those in our lives, and an appreciation for the joyous and plentiful things in life. On the shadow side, we see weakness in setting limits and boundaries for ourselves and others, thereby allowing cruelty and tyranny to go unchecked. Worst of all, from the perspective of the path of inner initiation, the shadow-magician of Chesed is the very definition of Crowley's "Black Brothers," clinging to the fruits of their mere personality and attainments, and forgetting the service to the universe that is such an integral part of any true ascent to Binah and beyond.

Here we need to pause and, in a sense, draw this part of our discussion to a close, since if we try to move beyond Chesed to the supernal triad of Binah, Chokmah, and Kether, we are forced to admit that these sephiroth don't have much to do with practical or psychological functioning. In fact, they don't pertain to everyday human consciousness at all. The most useful way to work with the supernals in this present context is simply to keep in mind that we should always be aspiring to the highest in ourselves, and in the universe, with service to all as the primary aim. As Crowley says in "One Star in Sight," the aspirant "must regard all his attainments as primarily the property of those less advanced aspirants who are confided to his charge."[2]

---

[2] In Crowley, A. (1997). *Magick: Liber ABA* (2nd rev. ed.). Hymenaeus Beta (Ed.). York Beach, ME: Red Wheel/Weiser, LLC, 495. [Note: I apologize for the relentlessly gendered language in the original quotations throughout this book.]

Even when there is no specifically identified problem, it is useful to make a pass through these sephiroth and perform a Qabalistic "check-up" on yourself—like preventive maintenance of your inner Tree of Life. Look at each sphere in its fullness and ask yourself how well you are living it out. Strive to catch the weak spots, the blind spots—the chinks in the psychological armor, so to speak. You can do more targeted interventions if you simply attend to what seems to be "off" in your life. Ponder the nature of the problem you're noticing, and see which sephirothic shadow side matches it.

Let's review an example. Suppose you are getting caught up in emotionality and living rather reactively, rather than executing more thoughtful and well-planned actions. It's difficult to think clearly because you are swept along with the waves of emotions. Once you can identify that's what is going on, you can easily see that it matches up with the shadow side of Netzach, as discussed above. A solution would be to look at Netzach in its fullness and consider how you might be able to take the intensity of the emotion you are feeling and put it in service to more constructive aims. Devote that intensity to your spiritual aspiration, for example, instead of to life issues which may actually require more thought than emotion. *Give that emotion something better to do*, so it doesn't feel so much like it needs to intrude into every other aspect of your life and assume control of it.

As another example, suppose you've noticed you are simply being a jerk. You are being too aggressive or irritable with people, perhaps engaging in bullying behavior (I'm looking at you, social media!), and people are giving you signals that you need to back off. Well, that sure sounds like Geburah's shadow side. You've got an excess of energy, force, and fire, but you need to find a constructive way to channel it. Look for areas of your life where you need to blast away obstacles that are legitimately in your way. Instead of getting irritable with your coworkers or your spouse and blasting *them* out of the way, look for places where you are dammed up, and try to live out Geburah in its fullness as you challenge those points of stuckness.

As I have discussed in *Living Thelema*[3] with regard to the selection of magical rituals, you can use invocations of the sephiroth to attune yourself to their energies, and bring in more of the force that you need to create balance. Too much Geburah? Try invoking Chesed and consecrating a talisman to keep with you for a while. Dry spell? Try invoking Netzach and performing a scrying in the resulting temple atmosphere; or boost the amount of devotional ritual in your daily life.

Exercise

I have created an exercise to augment and enrich your work with these tools. There are two goals here: to connect to the energies of each of the sephiroth and deepen your understanding of how they manifest in your life and consciousness; and conversely, to help you not *unduly* identify with any one of the sephiroth. For example, to avoid excessive focus on the physical body instead of your inner life, or to keep emotion flowing rather than getting too "in your head" about things, to not unduly to be bound up in the physical body or the mind or the emotions, and or so on.

Set aside a quiet space where you can be silent and undisturbed for at least 20 minutes. As always, have your magical diary ready so you can take notes after completing the exercise. I suggest you repeat it daily for a few weeks, to see how your awareness of these sephirothic aspects of self evolves. You may wish to record yourself reading these instructions, so you can free your mind to follow wherever the experience leads you without reference to written materials.

1. Find a comfortable and balanced posture, seated in a chair or in your favorite asana, or lying on a bed.

---

[3] Shoemaker, D. (2022). *Living Thelema: A Practical Guide to Attainment in Aleister Crowley's System of Magick.* Newburyport, MA: Weiser Books.

2. Bring your attention to your breathing. Note the passage of the air
   at the tip of your nose. The cool air moves in, and the warm and
   relaxing air moves out. Spend a few moments just focusing on this
   cycle of breath, keeping a gentle, easy rate and rhythm. Recite the
   following sentences to yourself. After each section, pause to meditate briefly on the truths communicated in these statements:

   i. *Malkuth*. I live in the physical world. I have a body with
      which I may experience this world and all its sensory wonders
      and pleasures. My senses are the eyes and ears of the universe,
      and through my life the universe witnesses and experiences
      itself. Yet, I am not my body.

   ii. *Yesod*. I see past the veil of matter to perceive the astral pat-
       terns underlying the physical world. The life-power flows
       through me as the force of my Will expressing itself in the
       boundless and ever-changing patterns of the unconscious
       mind. I wield this life-power in service of my own evolution,
       and in service to the evolution of humanity. Yet, I am not my
       mind, and I am not my astral body.

   iii. *Hod*. I possess an intellect with which I build conscious
        thoughts as cups of form, to give shape to the liquid of mag-
        ical force. I use reason and mental discipline to organize my
        life in service to the Will. Yet, I am not my intellect.

   iv. *Netzach*. I possess emotions as a fuel for aspiration and
       a medium for love. My soul yearns for the divine, and I
       enflame myself in prayer as I aspire to union with that which
       is beyond. Yet, I am not my emotions, and I am not my
       aspiration.

   v. *Tiphareth*. The light of my Holy Guardian Angel shines on
      the center of my being, from which I instruct and direct all
      the parts of myself in their right function. This center of

consciousness serves as the Prophet of my Holy Guardian Angel, whose voice is the True Will. Yet, I am more than this center of consciousness.

vi. *Geburah.* My True Will is an extension of universal will, and I construct my inner and outer life to be a perfect form for its expression. The power of all life is available to me in every moment. Yet, I am more than my Will.

vii. *Chesed.* I have consciousness of the path of my soul and the many lives I have lived before this one, and I govern my consciousness in the light of this knowledge. I strive in all things to live fully as an expression of the highest light. Yet, I am more than this.

viii. *Binah.* I have full consciousness of the Grail of holy blood into which the droplets of my individual lives have fallen, for I am that Grail. I have mingled my individual life with the universal life, and let go of all attachments of the small ego. I tend to the garden of my lower self with love and care. I receive my Word and give it birth. Yet, I am beyond the Grail.

ix. *Chokmah.* I bear the Word, the primal impulse of all the life of humanity. I am the universal will, all-powerful and infallible, the Lance that is plunged into the Grail of All. Yet, I am beyond the Lance and beyond the Word.

x. *Kether.* I am the One Source from which all things proceed, and to which all return. I am No Thing, yet in me is the potential for All Things that can exist. I am the primal point that sees every possibility, yet knows the unity of All. I AM.

3. Knowing that in truth, all of these points of awareness remain active and alive within you, return your consciousness to the present moment, and to your physical body.

4. Move your muscles and feel yourself fully engaged in your body, and in the physical world. Spend another few moments simply absorbing what you have experienced. Whenever you are ready, open your eyes.

CHAPTER 2

QABALISTIC PSYCHOLOGY IN THE NEW AEON

Part One: Introduction

In this multi-part chapter, we'll discuss the fundamentals of Qabalistic psychology. These concepts have been woven into much of the material I've covered in other writings and instruction, but I'll go into much more detail here than before. Importantly, this chapter will not merely review basic concepts like the Parts of the Soul, but will also give you a sense of why these are important for a Thelemic magician, in both theory and practice. Over the course of the chapter, we'll first examine individually the key Parts of the Soul: *nephesh*, *ruach*, and *neshamah*. We'll then conclude with a discussion of the implications of these concepts for sex magick (and indeed, *any* magick.) If you need a very basic primer on Qabalah itself, I suggest you review the first chapter of *Living Thelema*, or one of the many excellent modern books on the topic. I also suggest you review the "Sexual Magick and Sexual Mysticism" chapter in the earlier book, to lay the groundwork for what's presented in the final part of this chapter.

As a clinical psychologist and magician, exploring Qabalistic psychology was always inevitable for me. In fact, it was my "gateway" into Thelema and the magical path itself. When I was in graduate school in the early 1990s, I was studying the typical topics covered in many clinical psychology programs at the time—primarily cognitive-behavioral approaches to symptom reduction and behavior change. Though we surveyed all kinds of different theoretical orientations to therapy, such as classical Freudian, behavioral, Jungian, Adlerian, and so on, the fact is we weren't *deeply* trained in anything beyond cognitive-behavioral approaches. The so-called "depth psychology" theorists listed above, along with many others, were simply not in scientific "fashion"; and you certainly weren't going to find a chapter on Qabalistic psychology in one of the commonly available textbooks.[4] This left me feeling rather empty, and dry. I wanted a theory of life and of humanity that had space for mystery, wonder, and transpersonal aspects of life. I had been interested in the work of Carl Jung for many years, and I arranged a course of independent Jungian studies (book groups, discussions, etc.) with my primary professor and several classmates. I soon realized, however, that what I really wanted was a *personal* path of depth and mystery—a path of spiritual growth which I'd been actively resisting in my days as a more or less atheist undergraduate. Eventually I found my way to Israel Regardie's writings, and in particular his seminal book *The Middle Pillar*.[5]

In *The Middle Pillar*, which I highly recommend in any of its several editions, Regardie lays out the theory of Qabalistic psychology. He shows how it applies to the Tree of Life, and how it can be defined and understood in terms of our inner lives. This blew the top of my head off. Here

---

[4] As a sort of "completing of the circle," I later wrote what I believe to be the first chapter on Qabalistic psychology to appear in an undergraduate psychology textbook, published in the Instructor's Manual for James Fadiman and Robert Frager's *Personality and Personal Growth* (Pearson).

[5] Regardie, I. (2002). *The Middle Pillar: The Balance Between Mind and Magic* (3rd ed.). Chic & Sandra Tabatha Cicero (Eds.). St. Paul, MN: Llewellyn.

was a nuanced integration of Jungian theory and practice with Qabalistic tradition, capable of encompassing the mundane as well as the magical, the personal as well as the infinite. It was just what I needed, and I knew immediately that it would be my life's work.

So why is this system so useful and important for magicians? The answer is that the processes described in Qabalistic psychology, and the nuances of the system, allow us to understand and work with our inner lives at a higher degree of *specificity* than almost any other system I've encountered—even more than the depth psychology approaches taught in schools of psychotherapy such as those of Freud and Jung.

With Qabalistic psychology, we have a system that encompasses the entirety of the human psychospiritual constitution; but because it can be overlaid on the intricate paths and sephiroth on the Tree of Life, with all the profound mysteries they embody, we can build this psychological self-knowledge right into our understanding of the path of attainment itself. We can use the same language to describe the psyche that we use to describe our path of spiritual advancement, such as in an initiatory system like the A∴A∴ or the Temple of the Silver Star—essentially *any* system that is substantially based on the Tree of Life. Furthermore, the Qabalistic psychological model gives us insight into the nature of True Will. That is, it gives us an opportunity to understand the functioning of True Will as it manifests at all the levels of our psyche: unconsciously, consciously, and superconsciously. Importantly, when we understand the implications of the Qabalistic psychology model on our path of personal attainment and initiation, we can gain insight into how the human race itself should be evolving in the New Aeon. I'll use this fact as a "frame" as I discuss each Part of the Soul. We'll review the fullness of manifestation of each aspect of self in the New Aeon, as well as the "right relationship" *between* them when understood in light of Thelemic principles. In other words, what does the fully balanced, fully functional Thelemic magician look like when viewed through the lens of the Parts of the Soul?

Before I say anything more, however, I'd like to address a common criticism I've heard over the years when it comes to the overlap of psychology and magick. For some reason, when I discuss such things, people tend to assume I'm saying magick is "all in your head"; that I'm discounting the potential objective reality of spirits, gods, and angels or the prospect of "supernatural"-seeming magical processes themselves, or that I'm presenting a psychological model of understanding magick as if it's the only explanation, or the best explanation, for the phenomena under consideration. After all, in some of his early writings, even Crowley himself talked about the Goetic spirits as being "parts of the brain," although he later evolved to have a different perspective. My point here, however, is that we can have multiple perspectives on *any* field of study, can't we? The fields of biology and chemistry can teach us about the natural processes that allow humans to live, breathe, and engage in magical ritual. Mathematics has something to say about the underlying model of the Tree of Life. Yet, none of these perspectives argue that they are the *only* way to understand what they describe; and for some reason, when a mathematician or a chemist discusses their field in relation to magick, they aren't accused of reducing magick to numbers or chemical reactions. So when I talk about Qabalistic psychology, or frankly anything regarding the overlap of magic and psychology, I want it to be understood that I'm simply presenting one perspective on the matter; I am not saying that magical phenemena can be reductionistically described only in terms of psychology. The experiences I've had along my own magical path have led me to very different conclusions! I might also add that it's somewhat strange for someone to levy this sort of complaint against the Qabalistic psychology model, when the model *itself* contains the transpersonal and explicitly spiritual elements that a "magical" worldview typically requires. The Qabalistic psychology model in fact *demands* an understanding that there are superconscious realms of existence that go beyond the individual human psyche.

Let's move on to an examination of the Parts of the Soul. We're going to start with a brief overview of the Jungian model of the psyche, to define some useful terms that overlap closely with those of Qabalistic psychology. The Jungian model can thus serve as a convenient "jumping off place" for those new to Qabalistic psychology, especially when overlaid on the Tree of Life diagram. Jung himself never (to my knowledge) attempted to correlate his theories directly with the regions of the Tree of Life, so these are my own thoughts on the matter.

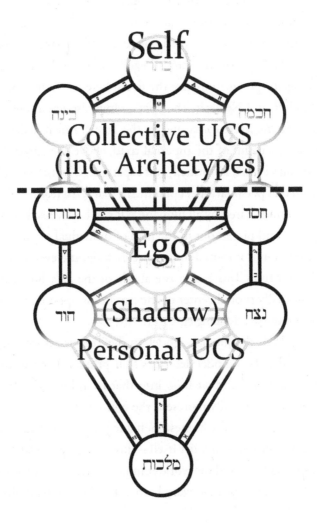

Malkuth is, of course, the physical body. Jung's *personal unconscious* includes aspects of the unconscious mind that are unique to our individual life: things we have experienced in our lives and then banished to the unconscious, things of which we've *never* been conscious, and things we're simply not thinking about consciously at the moment. I attribute the personal unconscious to the sphere of Yesod. The Jungian *ego* is the normal, conscious personality that thinks of itself as the "I" that goes out into the world and does things: I went to work, I drove the car, I have this kind of personality, I like this, I dislike this. Our memories, our intellect, our emotions, our intuition, and our senses—the ego comprises all of that. (Note that this is not a pejorative use of the word "ego," as we see in terms like "egotistical," "he's all ego," and so on.) On the Tree of Life, the Jungian ego encompasses the five spheres of Geburah, Chesed, Tiphareth, Hod, and Netzach. The unconscious also has a transpersonal aspect, the *collective unconscious*, and on the Tree of Life it makes sense to locate this in the realm of the supernal triad, above the Abyss. Like the personal unconscious, it is normally not experienced consciously; but it is distinct from that personal aspect of mind in that it is a realm of collective and *objective* mind shared by all humanity. It can be accessed via individual experience, and played out in the field of individual experience, consciously or not, but it is rooted in the species-wide, and even transhuman and universal, Mind. This is also the abode of the *Self*, Jung's term for the true, spiritually rooted center of the psyche, as opposed to the more superficial and outward-facing ego.

Having laid out the Jungian model on the Tree, let's move on to the Qabalistic model. This model describes four primary Parts of the Soul. Some have "subparts," and we'll go into that later, but these four basic Parts of the Soul essentially represent the entire spectrum of consciousness and existence, from the highest ineffable levels of cosmic consciousness and creative power—divinity itself—down to the physical world, the manifest physical body and the world it inhabits. The Qabalistic model is aligned with the concept that every human has within themselves a full

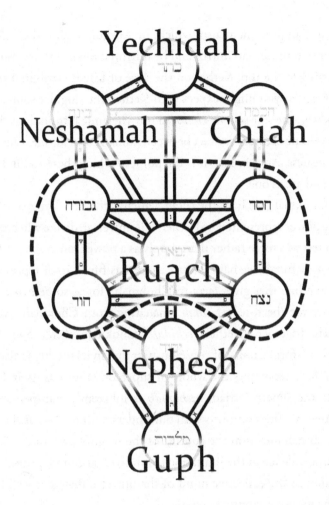

Yechidah

Neshamah ‖ Chiah

Ruach

Nephesh

Guph

Tree of Life. Human existence itself embodies a continuum of awareness, consciousness, and power that extends from the highest to the lowest levels of creation. I'm not using "high" or "low" as pejorative terms; "high" simply means something is closer to the ineffable aspects of pure spirit, and "low" means it is "denser" and closer to physical manifestation. This nuanced understanding of the continuum of consciousness in the universe, and therefore in ourselves, is one of the things that makes the Qabalistic psychology model so useful as a language for magicians. It implies many of the doctrines we hold to be true in terms of the function of a magician as a microcosm which, by working within the field of its own consciousness, can mirror and be mirrored by the macrocosm.

Starting at the top, Kether on the Tree of Life is attributed to *yechidah*. This is, as you might expect with Kether, the singular source of creative power, the star-self, or *khabs*, to use Thelemic terminology. It is the primary point of direct contact between human consciousness and divine consciousness. And, in fact, it is the point at which these are undifferentiated, and are as one.

At Chokmah, we have the *chiah*, which is the first "extension" of the creative power represented by Kether. It is universal, divine will beginning to manifest as a force rather than simply as a power source.

Then, at Binah, we have *neshamah*. Just as Binah itself represents the Understanding that gives *form* to Chokmah's force, so *neshamah* is the container for the force of *chiah* emanating from Chokmah. All three supernals together—Kether/*yechidah*, Chokmah/*chiah*, and Binah/*neshamah*—form a unity of consciousness that in its totality is also called *neshamah*. It represents the whole of superconsciousness itself. Since it involves the supernal triad, *neshamah* is inherently transpersonal and trans-Abyssal. This conforms with our understanding of what the attainment of Binah means in the context of the magical path of A∴A∴; that is, a transcendence of the limitations of individual consciousness, and an immersion in the collective mind of the universe that goes well beyond anything we've previously known.

The *ruach*, which means "breath," as in the breath of life and of consciousness, comprises the same five spheres as the Jungian ego—Chesed, Geburah, Tiphareth, Netzach, and Hod—and also (in many respects) Yesod. While the whole of the *ruach* thus includes the same functions of consciousness as the ego, the language of Qabalistic psychology allows a more nuanced and magically useful conception of how its "component parts" interrelate. The fact that it's centered in Tiphareth, for example, tells us something about the way the human mind takes in and organizes information. Tiphareth is like a communications hub, the spiritual center of consciousness that is constantly receiving inputs from all of the other spheres of the *ruach*: intellect (Hod), emotion (Netzach), memory (Chesed), will (Geburah), and intuition (Yesod). This is supplemented by sensory information gathered from Malkuth. (The Part of the Soul attributed to Malkuth, the physical senses and the physical body, is called the *guph*.) When all of this works as it should, it is the spiritually informed Tiphareth center which then directs our response to any given internal or external event.

The *nephesh*, sometimes called the "animal soul," includes characteristics of the less-conscious levels of the conscious mind, such as intuition, but primarily involves the same functions as the personal unconscious of Jung. It also includes instinctual drives, impulses, and autonomic functions. The term "animal soul" is apt, because the *nephesh* is that part of us which is living in a place of essentially animalistic consciousness—survival instincts, self-defensive mechanisms, and drives toward feeding and procreation. And in this sense, the *nephesh* is also what we might think of as the "inner child." I hate to use such a cliché, but it is indeed the child-like part of us, unrestricted by the higher reasoning and executive functions of the parent-like *ruach*. The *nephesh* is the child that needs to be nurtured, cared for, listened to, and prudently guided, but not suppressed or abused; the *ruach* is the adult that needs to function in the outer world and deal with other humans.

∴

In the remaining parts of this chapter, I'm going to tell you a story—a story about how the human race is evolving in the New Aeon of Thelema, and the implications of this evolution in terms of the relationships among the various Parts of the Soul. In systems of initiation (sometimes called "mystery schools") across the millennia, the intent has always been to aid in humanity's evolution. In whatever era they may have existed, they have always attempted to teach the *next step* in humanity's evolution. In the previous Aeon, I think it could be argued that this "next step" involved the cultivation of a fully functioning *ruach*. In the emergence of human civilization and culture, one of our greatest struggles has been recognizing that we don't have to live purely based on animal drives and instincts. For example, if something makes us feel angry, scared, or trapped and as a result we feel like punching somebody, *we don't have to.* We can pause, consider the consequences, and make a more thought-out decision. This higher reasoning is, of course, the controlling influence of the *ruach* on the *nephesh*. In the Old Aeon, a lot of humanity was in the initial phases of figuring that out. (And of course, many of us still wrestle with it quite often!)

This process of learning to control the *nephesh* was happening concurrently with the emergence of Christian cultures and beliefs, and the monolithic orthodoxies that sprang from them. The unfortunate solution offered was essentially, "Okay, *ruach*, if you want to control that bad little child-*nephesh* with all its urges toward sex, violence, and dirty things like that, you need God. You can't do it yourself." So exoteric Old Aeon religions taught ways of calling to an external force to help us master our own *nephesh*. In other words, we projected *neshamah* onto external deities, viewed as external sources of power, comfort, and safety, and then came to believe that the *only* way we could manage ourselves as individuals was through this external aid. The "savior" attribution to Jesus is perhaps the most prominent example of this: you can't just take care of yourself and be your own master, you need Jesus/God.

Now, at this point in human evolution, we've mostly got the *ruach* figured out. We understand the fight-or-flight response, and that we can calm our minds and relax our bodies when threatened, counteract the alarm response, and get into a less reactive state. Most of the time, in our day-to-day lives, we don't have any trouble being the cultured, civilized, controlled people we need to be to get along in the world.

But what is the next step *now*? What might human consciousness evolve into that would reflect a further development of the Parts of the Soul in relation to each other? We have established that the *ruach* can take care of the *nephesh*, and master some of those impulses—a "right relation-ship" between these two Parts of the Soul. When we look back on stages of humanity's existence where we *didn't* know that, it seems quite primi-tive, doesn't it? Well, I think humans a few centuries from now—perhaps even sooner—will experience the same sort of wonder and bemusement when they look back at *our* ignorance. Why didn't we understand that we are divine, creative beings with the power to shape our universe? Why didn't we perceive that we don't have to be subjected to a belief in, or oppression by, some imagined external deity that is our only hope for controlling ourselves? In other words, I believe the next step for human-ity's evolution involves forging the right relationship between *ruach* and *neshamah*.

We'll explore this story of human evolution in more detail throughout the remaining parts of this chapter. Along the way, we'll review the stages we move through along our individual paths of attainment and evolution, so that we can eventually get to that place where we are centered in *neshamah* as our core identity, and no longer limited by the faculties of the *ruach*.

Part Two: The Nephesh

As noted above, the *nephesh* is also known as the "animal soul" and encompasses our basic instincts, primal drives, sexual generativity, the autonomic nervous system, and aspects of the personal unconscious of Jung. In some models of the psyche, the *nephesh* is placed at the sphere of Yesod on the Tree of Life, and as such it has an intimate relationship with the process of initiatory advancement. Prior to attaining the Knowledge and Conversation of the Holy Guardian Angel (HGA), the primary way that information or communication from the Angel presents itself to our conscious mind is through the field of the unconscious; that is, through the realm of symbols which appear in dreams, in intuitions, or in our attending to "synchronicities" in our daily lives. Imagine Yesod/*nephesh* as the "lunar" subconsciousness that reflects the solar light of Tiphareth and the HGA into our conscious minds. The conscious mind looks down into that shadowy and highly symbolic field of awareness, and it becomes a conduit for communication from the Angel. The better we are at speaking that symbolic language, which is the "native tongue" of the *nephesh*, the more we are able to become conscious of the light of the HGA from Tiphareth and beyond. The HGA is whispering its wisdom to us at all times, long before full Knowledge and Conversation (K&C); our task is to *listen* the right way and pick up its instructions as best we can.

The placement of the *nephesh* at Yesod also shows us, through its proximity to Malkuth, the close relationship between the *nephesh* and the *guph*, or physical body. This is the oft-cited "mind-body connection" at its most hardwired and primal. Of all the Parts of the Soul, it is the *nephesh* which is most intimately attuned to, and in harmony with, the regulation of bodily processes like circadian rhythms, heart rate, and the breathing cycle. Thus, the wisdom of the body is most available to us when we are tuned in to the corresponding wisdom of subconsciousness.

Like every other aspect of consciousness, such as our intellect and our emotions, the *nephesh* and its intuitive truths are one source of data that the *ruach* can utilize to manage and govern the psyche. The *ruach* takes these signals, these "data points," from all of the senses and aspects of the psyche, and attempts to integrate them into a consolidated reality. It then makes decisions accordingly. As noted above, the *nephesh* is in many ways like the "child" aspect of consciousness. We begin our lives looking through its eyes, developing and expressing a primal, instinctual, and reactive way of living. This child-self tends to be much more in tune with all our senses, without much of the self-reflective consciousness associated with the *ruach*. So, if we think of the *nephesh* as the child aspect of consciousness, it's not hard to see the "child abuse" that has occurred over the course of several thousand years of Christian-influenced oppression—the body negativity and the suppression of freedom-seeking instincts that's been baked into our cultural experience within Western culture.

Accordingly, a lot of what we're going to discuss here in terms of the New Aeon evolution of the *nephesh* has to do with healing this Old Aeon abuse. This brings me to a model that I'll use throughout the remainder of this chapter: a three-part sequence of transformation that can be summarized as *purification, consecration,* and *initiation.*[6] When it comes to the healing of the *nephesh,* the operative stage is that of purification. We are purifying the life force and the body which is its vehicle; we are giving it an opportunity to live and come out and "play" without shame, without the body negativity and sex negativity that has been so endemic. The abused and neglected child-self can safely open its eyes and realize that in spite of millennia of targeted messaging, it's not a source of evil after all.

The inherent vulnerability of the *nephesh,* as of the newborn child, means that *fear* is ever-present. The child is unsure of its surroundings, and is trying to get its bearings: *How do I get around this place? How do I use my body? Who are these other giant people here? Can I trust them? After all, I'm depending on them for life, sustenance, and nurturance!* Accordingly, one of the ordeals of human development across history has been to cultivate a right relationship between the *nephesh* and the *ruach*; that is, to find a way to be the best *parent* we can be to our own child-selves. The *ruach* needs to parent the *nephesh* in a compassionate and nonjudgmental way—a way that clearly conveys to the *nephesh* that its instincts, its drives, its sexuality, its life force, are *all* divine and perfect. So, the purification stage involves the intentional washing away of the accretions of such negative Old Aeon influences. If we don't undergo this purification step, this wounded, vulnerable part of us will tend to reach out to unhealthy sources of perceived safety. This is one reason people become overly dependent on others for support or life-direction, when what they really need is to be more independent and trusting of themselves. Similarly, with misuse

---

[6] Some contemporary Thelemic initiatory systems include certain three-step degree sequences which, in my view, are expressions of the central formula under discussion here. Initiates of such traditions may wish to consult their own experience in this light while reading this chapter.

of substances, the aim is essentially to numb this primal fear, or at least forget about it for a while, through some sort of anesthetic process. When we cultivate the proper, healthy relationship between *ruach* and *nephesh*, we thereby *put our trust* in the right place.

There's another very important reason for purifying the *nephesh*: Thelemic magicians employ the life/sex force itself as a source of power. If we are (consciously or unconsciously) suffering from "neuroses" of the *nephesh*—the sex/body negativity and shame discussed above—it's definitely going to muddy the waters of every single bit of magick we do! If we walk into our temple to perform a ritual and there is a voice inside us, however small or distant, telling us that our bodies are evil or corrupt in some way, it sucks the force out of the very power source we are seeking to utilize. On the other hand, when we purify our understanding of the *nephesh*, recognizing its divine, creative nature, we can access its full power without it being tainted by those Old Aeon accretions of shame and negativity. Furthermore, we don't need an external savior if we are in ourselves divine, healthy, and complete—and this is yet another way in which this transformed understanding of the *nephesh* takes us out of the Old Aeon and into the New.

Part Three: The Ruach

As you will recall from Part One of this chapter, the *ruach* is the everyday consciousness of the psyche—the human personality in all its aspects, analogous to the Jungian ego. It is centered in Tiphareth, which itself functions as the central organizing principle of the psyche, taking in data from the senses, the intuition, the intellect, the emotions, and more, and synthesizing this into a meaningful interpretation of reality. It is thus the *ruach* that serves as our primary interface between our inner world and the macrocosm that surrounds us. For a ritualized example of this last point, consider the role of the Deacon in the Gnostic Mass.

The Deacon serves in the spiritual and ineffable realm of the action of the Mass, while simultaneously functioning as a sort of "emcee" of the social aspects of ritual, leading the congregation as they move through the ritual.

In the pre-Adepthood stage of the path of initiation, the *ruach* tends to perceive itself as a separate being from the outer world (and thus from other *ruachs*) so that it may interact with them in a functional manner. It maintains this "delusion of separateness" as a necessary tool for external, practical life and for processing mental data, while remaining mostly oblivious to trans-egoic realms (i.e., above the Abyss) where the unity of all things is directly perceived. While maintaining its connection to the outer world, the *ruach* must at the same time be sensitive and responsive to inner stimuli impinging upon it via senses, intuition, thoughts, and feelings. It must also strive to perceive material sprouting up through the subconscious field of the *nephesh,* the personal unconscious, through dreams, symbols, synchronicities, and other flashes of spiritual truth. Finally, the *ruach* must attempt to interpret signals from the physical body, including (importantly) the autonomic nervous system's messages of alarm/danger or, alternatively, relaxation and safety.

Clearly, the *ruach* has a big job, and it's not one to be dispensed with as we walk the path of inner transformation. There is much talk of the "destruction of the ego" in some systems, and this may sound nice in the context of our strivings to unite with the higher aspects of self. Yet in actuality, we can never do without the *ruach* as long as we are incarnate humans. Even someone who has crossed the Abyss and attained the grade of Magister Templi, aware of higher truth, non-dual reality, and the falsity of separateness, must continue to interact functionally with the outer world. If they cannot, they are likely evidencing psychosis rather than true mastery.

Consider Crowley's words in his essay on skepticism, "The Soldier and the Hunchback," with regard to the relationship of the physical human to the spiritual human; that is, of Malkuth to Kether, and the role of Tiphareth in regard to lower realities:

> *Ah! let me introduce you to the man in Tiphereth; that is, the man who is trying to raise his consciousness from Malkuth to Kether.*

> *This Tiphereth man is in a devil of a hole! He knows theoretically all about the Kether point of view (or thinks he does) and practically all about the Malkuth point of view. Consequently he goes about contradicting Malkuth; he refuses to allow Malkuth to obsess his thought. He keeps on crying out that there is no difference between a goat and a God, in the hope of hypnotising himself (as it were) into that perception of their identity, which is his (partial and incorrect) idea of how things look from Kether.*

> *This man performs great magic; very strong medicine. He does really find gold on the midden and skeletons in pretty girls.*

> *In Abiegnus the Sacred Mountain of the Rosicrucians the Postulant finds but a coffin in the central shrine; yet that coffin contains Christian Rosencreutz who is dead and is alive for evermore and hath the keys of Hell and of Death.*

> *Ay! your Tiphereth man, child of Mercy and Justice, looks deeper than the skin!*

> *But he seems a ridiculous object enough both to the Malkuth man and to the Kether man.*

> *Still, he's the most interesting man there is; and we all must pass through that stage before we get our heads really clear, the Kethervision above the Clouds that encircle the mountain Abiegnus.*[7]

---

[7] Crowley, A. (1993). *The Equinox*, Vol. I, No. 1. York Beach, ME: Weiser, 126–7.

In the discussion of the *nephesh* earlier in this chapter, I emphasized the importance of its task in the New Aeon—learning where to turn for appropriate nurturance and guidance; that is, to the *ruach*, its rightful and natural "parent." In addition to this role as parent of the *nephesh*, the *ruach* manages the relationships between ourselves and other people (i.e., other *ruachs*). All too often, we become unheathily dependent on other people, and allow (or even, unfortunately, encourage) them to be unduly dependent on us. The New Aeon evolution of these patterns involves overturning ego traps such as false pride, social insecurity, and impulses to control others, and finding a right relationship of *ruach* to *ruach*. We enlist appropriate aid from those we trust, and by offering our own aid in return, a coequal and mature *inter*dependence results.

Let's review what's happening in our three-stage process of New Aeon purification, consecration, and initiation with regard to the *ruach*. We've seen that the *nephesh* was purified as Old Aeon sex- and body-negative obsessions were metaphorically washed away. Here, however, we are at the consecration stage, where the purified self is put in harmony with, and given power by, divine aims. What part of us might be in a position to detect and interpret those divine aims? The *ruach*! A properly functioning *ruach* is the part of us that is able to have enough awareness of all of the inner and outer stimuli—and sufficient glimpses of True Will—to make right choices in life. And "right choices aligned with True Will" is one important way of understanding what true spiritual consecration is: a purified human soul that is then given its right trajectory in the cosmos, in accordance with True Will.

One of the additional, inevitable pitfalls of the *ruach*, prior to its evolution through initiatory attainment, is thinking it's the "boss" of the Self—the one running the show. After several thousand years of humanity working hard to develop the *ruach*, it thinks pretty highly of itself! We humans lose sight of the fact that the real spiritual core of ourselves is not this mere center of personality. Gaining awareness of the actual truth takes some serious inner work, whether that's done through psychotherapy or other self-analysis, or through explicitly magical and mystical practices. In any case, one of the central tasks of the *ruach* in the New Aeon is to "get over itself" a little bit. It must perceive that it's *not* actually the one in charge, in the deepest sense. If we boil down the New Aeon evolution of the *ruach* to a few key phrases, it might look something like: "Grow up," "Mind your own business," "Help others without hurting yourself," and "Don't confuse the mastery of your personality and your outer life with being the real master of your soul." This true master is, of course, the *neshamah*, which we will explore in more detail in the next part of this chapter.

Crowley left us many essays, initiatory rituals, and other resources that teach us about the right functioning of the *ruach*, but perhaps one of the most prominent is *Liber Libræ*, "The Book of the Balance," which is itself a development of an earlier lecture. Crowley encountered the Hermetic Order of the Golden Dawn in the form of a "charge" during initiation. A charge is a moral instruction not presented as an oath, or as a component of dramatic ritual. As such, a charge is designed to be heard by the initiate in a ritually intensified state of awareness—alert *ruach*-consciousness, if you will; ready to take in information, make decisions about its import, and integrate it with other data, whether intellectual, emotional, intuitive, sensory, or from higher spiritual sources. Let's review some of the *ruach* instructions from *Liber Libræ*,[8] line by line.

> 0. *Learn first—Oh thou who aspirest unto our ancient Order!—that Equilibrium is the basis of the Work. If thou thyself hast not a sure foundation, whereon wilt thou stand to direct the forces of Nature?*

The *ruach* must learn to make decisions about how to live in a balanced way. As discussed earlier, it is centered in Tiphareth, and must take in information from all the different "data sources" of the human psyche

---

[8] Crowley, A. (1993). *The Equinox*, Vol. I, No. 1. York Beach, ME: Weiser, 17–21.

and the surrounding world. Only then can it rightly choose and direct the actions of the human, writ large.

> *1. Know then, that as man is born into this world amidst the Darkness of Matter, and the strife of contending forces; so must his first endeavour be to seek the Light through their reconciliation.*

The *ruach* is charged with the incredibly important duty of seeing past the duality implicit in all of our experiences in Malkuth, to seek the light that is coming from beyond, and to find the reconciliation of these apparent opposites, such as good vs. evil, matter vs. spirit, self vs. other.

> *2. Thou then, who hast trials and troubles, rejoice because of them, for in them is Strength, and by their means is a pathway opened unto that Light.*

All too often, we judge the "goodness" of something based solely (and reflexively) on whether we (i.e., the *ruach*) like it or not. Quite simply, "trials and troubles" are things the *ruach* doesn't like, and triumphs are things that it likes. On its own plane, this is all fine and dandy, but to evolve the *ruach* must learn that initiation comes just as often from unpleasant experiences as pleasant ones. (The Devil Atu of the Tarot is one useful symbol of this universal truth.)

> *3. How should it be otherwise, O man, whose life is but a day in Eternity, a drop in the Ocean of time; how, were thy trials not many, couldst thou purge thy soul from the dross of earth?*
>
> *Is it but now that the Higher Life is beset with dangers and difficulties; hath it not ever been so with the Sages and Hierophants of the past? They have been persecuted and reviled, they have been tormented of men; yet through this also has their Glory increased.*

Human life as experienced by the *ruach* is transitory and often painful. Truth lies beyond, in the realm of the spirit and the *neshamah*.

> *4. Rejoice therefore, O Initiate, for the greater thy trial the greater thy Triumph. When men shall revile thee, and speak against thee falsely, hath not the Master said, "Blessed art thou!"?*

> *5. Yet, oh aspirant, let thy victories bring thee not Vanity, for with increase of Knowledge should come increase of Wisdom. He who knoweth little, thinketh he knoweth much; but he who knoweth much hath learned his own ignorance. Seest thou a man wise in his own conceit? There is more hope of a fool, than of him.*

This reads like a stern lecture to the *ruach* concerning the vanity of its belief that it's running the show, or that it knows the truth in any but a mundane sense.

> *6. Be not hasty to condemn others; how knowest thou that in their place, thou couldest have resisted the temptation? And even were it so, why shouldst thou despise one who is weaker than thyself?*

The *ruach* is reminded of the principle of psychological projection. When we're pointing our fingers at someone and accusing them of some frailty or fault, we are probably ignoring a similar blind spot in ourselves.

> *7. Thou therefore who desirest Magical Gifts, be sure that thy soul is firm and steadfast; for it is by flattering thy weaknesses that the Weak Ones will gain power over thee. Humble thyself before thy Self, yet fear neither man not spirit. Fear is failure, and the forerunner of failure: and courage is the beginning of virtue.*

> *8. Therefore fear not the Spirits, but be firm and courteous with them; for thou hast no right to despise or revile them; and this too may lead thee astray. Command and banish them,*

curse them by the Great Names if need be; but neither mock
nor revile them, for so assuredly wilt thou be led into error.

Interpreted intrapsychically, this can be seen as an instruction to the *ruach* about how to treat the *nephesh*. We are to be firm but courteous, not despising or reviling it. We keep it in control, helping it understand that its impulses are important and sacred, but they can't often make the final decision concerning how the entirety of the psyche behaves. (This intrapsychic interpretation does not, of course, invalidate this passage's relevance to relations with external spirits.)

> *9. A man is what he maketh himself within the limits fixed by*
> *his inherited destiny; he is a part of mankind; his actions affect*
> *not only what he calleth himself, but also the whole universe.*

> *10. Worship and neglect not, the physical body which is thy*
> *temporary connection with the outer and material world.*
> *Therefore let thy mental Equilibrium be above disturbance by*
> *material events; strengthen and control the animal passions,*
> *discipline the emotions and the reason, nourish the Higher*
> *Aspirations.*

Again, the Tiphareth-centered *ruach* takes in and integrates information from all the parts of the psyche and the physical world, before formulating right actions in response.

> *11. Do good unto others for its own sake, not for reward, not for*
> *gratitude from them, not for sympathy. If thou art generous,*
> *thou wilt not long for thine ears to be tickled by expressions of*
> *gratitude.*

This is a charge to the *ruach* in regard to its propensity for vanity, presumption, and the desire for flattery.

> *12. Remember that unbalanced force is evil; that unbal-*
> *anced severity is but cruelty and oppression; but that also*

*unbalanced mercy is but weakness which would allow and
abet Evil. Act passionately; think rationally; be Thyself.*

13. True ritual is as much action as word; it is Will.

*14. Remember that this earth is but an atom in the universe,
and that thou thyself art but an atom thereon, and that
even couldst thou become the God of this earth whereon thou
crawlest and grovellest, that thou wouldest, even then, be but
an atom, and one amongst many.*

Ouch! Again, keeping the ego in check. Also, note the tripartite
charge corresponding to the Parts of the Soul, and describing their
right functions: act passionately (*nephesh*); think rationally (*ruach*);
be Thyself (*neshamah*).

*15. Nevertheless have the greatest self-respect, and to that end
sin not against thyself. The sin which is unpardonable is know-
ingly and wilfully to reject truth, to fear knowledge lest that
knowledge pander not to thy prejudices.*

The *ruach* must not allow its likes and dislikes (i.e., "prejudices") to
act as a perceptual filter that limits its ability to take in *all* data from the
universe; if it succumbs to this tendency, horrendous personality imbalances are inevitable.

*16. To obtain Magical Power, learn to control thought;
admit only those ideas that are in harmony with the end
desired, and not every stray and contradictory Idea that presents itself.*

*17. Fixed thought is a means to an end. Therefore pay attention
to the power of silent thought and meditation. The material act
is but the outward expression of thy thought, and therefore hath
it been said that "the thought of foolishness is sin." Thought is*

the commencement of action, and if a chance thought can pro-
duce much effect, what cannot fixed thought do?

Here we learn about the training of the mind to focus, through yoga and similar practices, and to maintain that focus, and fine tune it so it is in line with magical aims and, eventually and most importantly, with True Will.

> *18. Therefore, as hath already been said, Establish thyself firmly in the equilibrium of forces, in the centre of the Cross of the Elements, that Cross from whose centre the Creative Word issued in the birth of the Dawning Universe.*

> *19. Be thou therefore prompt and active as the Sylphs, but avoid frivolity and caprice; be energetic and strong like the Salamanders, but avoid irritability and ferocity; be flexible and attentive to images like the Undines, but avoid idleness and changeability; be laborious and patient like the Gnomes, but avoid grossness and avarice.*

This is the Tiphareth-centered *ruach* as the crowning point of the pentagram, showing its presidency over the four elements as an emissary of the spirit. The elements are named here in the form of their corresponding elemental beings: Sylphs (air), Salamanders (fire), Undines (water), and Gnomes (earth).

> *20. So shalt thou gradually develop the powers of thy soul, and fit thyself to command the Spirits of the elements. For wert thou to summon the Gnomes to pander to thine avarice, thou wouldst no longer command them, but they would command thee. Wouldst thou abuse the pure beings of the woods and mountains to fill thy coffers and satisfy thy hunger of Gold? Wouldst thou debase the Spirits of Living Fire to serve thy wrath and hatred? Wouldst thou violate the purity of the Souls*

of the Waters to pander to thy lust of debauchery? Wouldst
thou force the Spirits of the Evening Breeze to minister to thy
folly and caprice? Know that with such desires thou canst but
attract the Weak, not the Strong, and in that case the Weak
will have power over thee.

21. In the true religion there is no sect, therefore take heed that
thou blaspheme not the name by which another knoweth his
God; for if thou do this thing in Jupiter thou wilt blaspheme
יהוי and in Osiris יהשוי. Ask and ye shall have! Seek, and ye
shall find! Knock, and it shall be opened unto you!

Liber Libræ concludes by reinforcing the importance of not letting our prejudices or mundane ego-strivings impair our choice of right action.

Part Four: The Neshamah

The *neshamah* comprises those transpersonal and superconscious aspects of the psyche corresponding to the supernal triad on the Tree of Life. As mentioned earlier in the chapter, *neshamah* is the term applied both to Binah specifically and to the entirety of the supernal triad, and the latter is the primary way I'll be using the term here. This supernal consciousness transcends our everyday egoic strivings, wants, and desires and contains archetypes, spiritual ideals, and symbolic material in its highest forms. It's an entirely transpersonal and spiritual component of the human psyche; or, perhaps more properly stated, it is the eternal spiritual core of the psyche which which we can, with training, come into contact. The *neshamah* has always been, and always will be, beyond the *ruach*. In fact, when we speak of crossing the Abyss on the Path of Return, what's really happening is that we're getting in touch with the part of us that *has always been there.* As with most "journey" metaphors we encounter in our work as magicians, the reality is more about "getting your head in the right place" than "going" anywhere. We don't "find" the *neshamah*; we simply remember how to speak to it directly and consciously, rather than through the hazy lens of the personal unconscious and its symbolic language.

Throughout this chapter, I've been describing the creation of a "talisman" of sorts, via a process of purification, consecration, and initiation. This talisman is, of course, *ourselves* as fully spiritually functioning human beings, living from a place of empowerment by instincts and drives, but with these uplifted and directed in accordance with True Will by the *neshamah*-informed *ruach*. Our task as Adepts, post K&C, is to stay consciously plugged into this power source as much as possible—after all, it is the *neshamah* that is the real source of awareness of True Will, via our conscious contact with the HGA. In our work with the *nephesh*, the talisman underwent a purification of those Old Aeon accretions of sex negativity and body negativity that had suppressed our free-flowing and unashamed expression of life energy. Next, in our work with the *ruach*, we consecrated the talisman, focusing our intention to select magical aims and make wise choices about our life course, in harmony with True Will. Now, we're ready for the final charging of the talisman, completing our "initiation" as balanced human beings, fully empowered by the divine creative force resident in each of us.

As with all important thresholds of growth, there's an ordeal involved, and the ordeal here is one of embracing, not merely tolerating, the transient nature of the individual human life and personality. We are in truth immortal beings, yet this immortality does not belong to the human personality, but to the *khabs*, the star-self that is the real core of who we are. If we root our identity in the *ruach*, we become lost in the sorrow of grieving the transient shell of our human lives and bodies; but if we identify with the *neshamah*, we recognize our experience as an eternal adventure of ongoing evolution, undulating like the coils of a serpent through life and death, as Crowley has put it.

In this sense, our work of final initiation here involves forging the right relationship between the *ruach* and the *neshamah*, in accord with New Aeon consciousness. As with each of the other Parts of the Soul, there is a specific New Aeon evolution of this relationship: namely, to increasingly identify with superconsciousness as the core of who we are, and to allow the "death" of the ego/*ruach*. This death is an overturning of the *ruach*'s assumptions about its place in the picture, not an actual destruction. The *ruach* makes self-serving attempts throughout our lives to usurp the *neshamah*'s rightful rulership, but like it or not, it always ends up being put back in its place. We all have countless examples of getting our egos busted, to be sure. When we get off track, when the ego thinks it's really in the driver's seat, and it's trying to steer us in a direction at odds with True Will, we tend to get a pretty brisk slap in the face from the universe. When this happens, we may feel as though we're being knocked off our path, since things aren't going according to the *ruach*'s plans, but in actuality we're being knocked *back onto it*.

To understand the specific nature of the New Aeon right relationship between *ruach* and *neshamah*, let's start by briefly reviewing what happened between the *ruach* and *nephesh* in the Old Aeon. You'll recall that the *ruach* needed to be trained to take dominion over the *nephesh*—to be its rightful parent—so that we could transcend mere animal drives. After a few millennia of humanity working on this, we're all pretty well aware that we are more than these drives, and that we are not obligated to act on them without reflection. That was the Old Aeon lesson the *ruach* needed to learn. The problem was that the solution offered in Judeo-Christian culture—submitting ourselves to an imaginary daddy-god that would save us—was, shall we say, problematic. In any case, in retrospect we can see the silliness of thinking that we were merely reactive animals, slaves to our own impulses, without an ability to govern our own behavior.

Now imagine 500 years from now, when we look back on the *current* state of human awareness. What belief structures will seem similarly outdated and simplistic to us from that vantage point? As I suggested at the beginning of this chapter, it seems to me that the central mystery needing to be unveiled is the truth of the divine creative power resident in every human. That is, future humans will look back in bemusement that 21st-century humanity had not yet grasped the reality of its own godhead: "Those silly humans, trapped in the belief that they *were* their personalities!" Our New Aeon lesson is to embrace this godhead (embodied by the *neshamah*) in all its aspects. We don't need to transcend some sinful or unholy aspect of self. We don't need to rely on some external redeemer to raise us up or save us—there's nothing we need to be redeemed from! And we can *raise ourselves up* from our sorry state of ego-absorption, once we've realized that the *neshamah,* not the *ruach,* is the real Master on the throne of our inner temple. *Every* part of us is sacred. To paraphrase our exclamation at the conclusion of the Gnostic Mass, there is no part of us that is not of the Gods. All those impulses that we used to suppress and call evil and shameful are in fact life-affirming sources of power. We simply need to harness them and direct them according to our best understanding of True Will, by forging a right relationship to *neshamah.* Once the New Aeon is realized in its fullness, humanity will be a race of beings that, by and large, live each day from a place of this evolved awareness of our divine nature.

Part Five: Implications for Sex Magick

If we accept the premises above concerning the right functioning and divine nature of a New Aeon human being, how might we translate this self-understanding into a course of action that fully utilizes all the power sources available to us? Certainly, such a fully empowered human is well positioned to conduct powerful magical ritual. Our specific attention might be drawn, however, to sex magick, since the free-flowing utilization of the sex/life force is one of the key benefits of New Aeon consciousness. This is, of course, one of the most important technical aspects of Crowley's magical work, and one I've discussed at some length in the relevant chapter of *Living Thelema.* (I'll reiterate my earlier recommendation that you review that chapter before continuing here.) In contrast to the approach in that earlier work, in the remainder of this chapter I'll tie together the underlying Qabalistic psychology model with the practical execution of a sexual magick ritual, demonstrating that this sort of ritual approach is actually a natural and full extension of the deepest implications of the Qabalistic model itself. It is, in fact, the birthright of the New Aeon human being.

To do the most powerful magick possible (taking a tip from *Liber Libræ* once again), we need to be able to do that act passionately, think rationally about how we're doing it, and execute it in a state of connection with the deepest spiritual sources of power, in accordance with True Will (i.e., "Be thyself"). In terms of our three-stage process, in order to have unfettered power from the *nephesh*, we must have purified our relationship to our own sex force so that it is free of any accretions which detract from its true sacred nature. We must have sharpened our control of the *ruach* and consecrated it to divine aims, so that we are truly able to *direct* the sex force toward any desired magical aim. We have strengthened the muscles of our capacity to focus. We have diligently trained ourselves with yoga, and built our inner catalog of symbols such that we can effectively invoke and harness the desired magical force in a specific and efficient way. We have trained the *ruach* to "fall in love" with any desired idea, and to direct the force of our devotion in its direction. The essence of sex magick is that we are working with forces typically associated with love or lust for another human, but instead directing them toward a magical aim with the same degree of intensity. Finally, in the initiation phase connected with *neshamah*, we have to synthesize these last two processes into a workable approach to sexual magick. We must ensure to the best of our ability that the aims of the work are in accordance with True Will, and empowered by a connection to the highest source of spiritual force in *neshamah*. Only when we have the primal power of *nephesh*, the directing and focusing abilities of *ruach*, and the spiritual linkage of *neshamah* all working together can we really do sex magick, or any magick, with full efficacy. Thus empowered, the magician can truly exercise dominion over microcosm *and* macrocosm, thereby "pronouncing" the Tetragrammaton (הוהי) in all the Four Worlds (Atziluth-Briah-Yetzirah-Assiah) simultaneously.

Now let's discuss sexual magick in the specific context of what we've learned about Qabalistic psychology. For convenience, we'll break this down into five steps:

1. We are aligned with the True Will via linkage to *neshamah*, and plugged into that power source by virtue of our connection to the HGA.

2. We (at the *ruach* level) have chosen a magical aim in alignment with our best understanding of True Will, and with certainty of the necessity of the aim coming to fruition. The *ruach* maintains awareness that it is merely a conduit for the flow of universal force, not the power source itself. The *ruach* formulates the magical aim as simply and concisely as possible, condensing this into what we'll call a "Will-Seed." In any magical ritual, certainly including a sexual magick ritual, we must sharpen our focus on the desired aim into a concise-enough symbolic *form* such that we can easily maintain sufficient awareness of it of throughout the ritual, but especially at its climax. This allows us to impress the Will-Seed on the object of the working—typically a talisman, magical implement, or eucharist.

3. The generative fire of *nephesh*, the creative life force itself, is stoked via sexual activity while maintaining a "background" awareness of the magical aim.

4. At the climax of the ritual, the resulting *nepheshic* force is released. The Will-Seed flows toward the magical object carried by the resolute focus of the *ruach*, and with linkage to *neshamah*, the HGA, and True Will guiding its trajectory.

5. With the aim of the working still strongly in focus, the participants mindfully and ritually complete the charging of the

talisman or magical implement, and/or consume the eucharist. The Will-Seed is thus "planted" in the fertile soil of the consciousness of the participants.[9]

The fundamental magical action is this: At the moment of orgasm, the Will-Seed is released from that present moment of ego-death to take root in the *next* moment. That is, at the climax of any ritual the magician essentially "dies" (in relation to their former sense of self) and in the next moment they are "reborn" into a reality that *embodies* the previously designed Will-Seed. Regardless of whether the ritual is designed to create a change of consciousness, a change in our own nature, or a change in our outer circumstances, we must let go of the old in order to formulate the new. The newly born magician is in this sense a fertile patch of soil, ready to implant the Will-Seed in themselves and implement it.

Conclusion

I encourage you to consider all these points in the light of your existing self-knowledge, your best understanding of your True Will, and your goals for personal and spiritual growth. It is my hope that by building a deeper and more nuanced understanding of your own psychospiritual makeup, you will be enabled to bring the maximum degree of power, focus, and spiritual integrity to all of your magick.

Act passionately; think rationally; be Thyself.

---

[9] Such a ritual could easily be adapted as a solo working, or with one or more partners. Obviously, all participants should exercise appropriate hygienic and safety precautions, and must have expressed full consent for all proceedings. All of this will vary greatly depending on the people and the situation, so I will simply advise common sense. I would also like to emphasize that in my experience, the formulae of sexual magick presented here (in rough outline) can be effectively worked by anyone, regardless of sexual or gender identity. The real keys to the method are energetic, not anatomical or biochemical, and involve capacities residing in every human being.

CHAPTER 3

ON THE NATURE OF EVIL
AND THE SHADOW SIDE
OF THE MAGICIAN

Philosophers, theologians, politicians, psychologists, and seemingly everyone else have debated the nature of evil for millennia. In this chapter, I will summarize a few perspectives on the question, and then present a Thelemic model of understanding it, as implied in Crowley's writings and related source documents. I'll also review how these ideas can be employed in a magical and initiatory context to transform the self, and how we might employ concepts like the Jungian "shadow" in psychological work to address these issues.

The Judeo-Christian model has overshadowed (figurative pun intended) much of the thinking about evil in the Western world for centuries. In an oversimplified nutshell, it views evil as a universal force of nature that actively opposes and undermines a fairly specific code of assumed virtues, both in society and in the individual. Evil is defined as a force that is, by its nature, seen to overturn, undermine, or erode a certain set of values that are predefined by one group or another (usually the people who have money and power). This force is often personified, which is how we get an idea like the Christian "devil"—a sort of evil god that embodies the force of evil itself. This narrow-minded and limiting view, in any given culture, subculture, or individual, tends to boil down to this: Evil is anything that scares me, or goes against my own sense of what is right.

On the psychological plane, this results in the projection of our own perceptions of evil onto other individuals, cultures, ideas, or "foreign" deities. Crowley even comments on this in *Magick in Theory and Practice*, Chapter 21, when he says, "The devil is, historically, the God of any people that one personally dislikes."[10] We thereby project our "shadow"—the underexplored and disowned aspects of ourselves—onto others, as something like a psychological "pressure release valve." When societies as a whole do this, true horrors emerge, expressed in attitudes toward others who are of the wrong religion, the wrong color, the wrong political leaning, and so on. By labeling *them* as the bad guys, we disown our own inner bad guy. The problem with this, psychologically (and I think this is where the *real* evil lies), is that by repressing aspects of our own psyches or culture that we unconsciously dislike, we commit a crime against nature. We limit ourselves, and indeed our humanity, by attempting to wall off this part of ourselves and label it as unacceptable. We don't acknowledge it, we don't work with it, and we don't find the *divinity* in it.

This brings us to the view of evil in Thelema, which according to Crowley can be summarized as the "sin" of restricting the True Will. What are the implications of this? Firstly, there is no predetermined code of laws concerning what is good or evil. A Thelemite cannot, in my view, say that it is *always* wrong to do activity X, because there is no law in Thelema that says that. There's just one commandment, not ten, which is

---

[10] Crowley, A. (1997). *Magick: Liber ABA* (2nd rev. ed.). Hymenaeus Beta (Ed.). York Beach, ME: Red Wheel/Weiser, LLC, 277.

to do one's True Will. Thelema thus posits a relativistic and situational, not absolute and immutable, view of evil. Yet, we can see various places in Crowley's writings—for example, in his essay "Duty"—where he elaborates on the interpersonal and societal implications of living according to True Will. It's definitely not a matter of " do whatever you want"! There are no set laws of right and wrong, but there are certainly *implications* of right and wrong that follow directly from the central law of Thelema. Here are some excerpts from "Duty":

> *Abstain from all interferences with other wills. "Beware lest any force another, King against King!" [AL II:24[11]] . . . To seek to dominate or influence another is to seek to deform or destroy him; and he is a necessary part of one's own Universe, that is, of one's self. . . .*

> *The essence of crime is that it restricts the freedom of the individual outraged. (Thus, murder restricts his right to live; robbery, his right to enjoy the fruits of his labour; coining, his right to the guarantee of the state that he shall barter in security; etc.) It is then the common duty to prevent crime by segregating the individual, and by the threat of reprisals; also, to teach the criminal that his acts, being analyzed, are contrary to his own True Will. (This may often be accomplished by taking from him the right which he has denied to others; as by outlawing the thief, so that he feels constant anxiety for the safety of his own possessions, removed from the ward of the State.) The rule is quite simple. He who violated any right declares magically that it does not exist; therefore it no longer does so, for him. . . .*

---

[11] Chapter II, verse 24 in Crowley, A. (1991). *The Law Is for All*. Israel Regardie (Ed.). Phoenix: New Falcon Publications.

Apply the Law of Thelema to all problems of fitness, use, and development. It is a violation of the Law of Thelema to abuse the natural qualities of any animal or object by diverting it from its proper function, as determined by consideration of its history and structure. Thus, to train children to perform mental operations, or to practice tasks, for which they are unfitted, is a crime against nature. Similarly, to build houses of rotten material, to adulterate food, to destroy forests, etc., etc., is to offend.[12]

We can find further teachings regarding the Thelemic view of evil in one of its Holy Books, *Liber Tzaddi*, although they are not explicitly presented as such:

36. Many have arisen, being wise. They have said 'Seek out the glittering Image in the place ever golden, and unite yourselves with It.'

37. Many have arisen, being foolish. They have said, 'Stoop down unto the darkly splendid world, and be wedded to that Blind Creature of the Slime.'

38. I who am beyond Wisdom and Folly, arise and say unto you: achieve both weddings! Unite yourselves with both!

39. Beware, beware, I say, lest ye seek after the one and lose the other!

40. My adepts stand upright; their head above the heavens, their feet below the hells.

41. But since one is naturally attracted to the Angel, another to the Demon, let the first strengthen the lower link, the last attach more firmly to the higher.

---

[12] Crowley, A. "Duty" (various publications).

42. Thus shall equilibrium become perfect. I will aid my dis-
ciples; as fast as they acquire this balanced power and joy so
faster will I push them.[13]

It seems to me (and this is simply one person's opinion) that the first couple of lines, "Seek out the glittering Image" vs. "Stoop down unto the darkly splendid world," imply that there is divinity, power, and purpose in *all* things. When the Book says, "achieve both weddings! Unite yourselves with both!" it seems to be impelling us to expand ourselves to the fullest; to embrace all of these forms of experience and being, and not limit ourselves to that to which we are naturally drawn. "Beware I say, lest ye seek after the one and lose the other" and "My adepts stand upright, their head above the heavens, their feet below the hells" seem to describe a Thelemic Adept as someone who has fully embraced earthly, mundane, or even dark-seeming experiences, as well as those embodying the highest light.

While there is great wisdom in the statements regarding the balance between the "angel" and the "demon," we can see in the way Crowley structured the system of A∴A∴ that *timing* makes a difference; the central and supreme task from the grades of Probationer through Adeptus Minor is to forge the strongest possible link to the HGA. In any case, the aspirant is certainly confronted with the depths of their own unconscious mind, full of wonder and possibility, but also eliciting the fear of facing the unknown. It is useful to remember that the root word for "hell" refers to a "concealed place," and we can understand the human unconscious mind to be a primary example of such a hidden or unknown place. The actual danger is from the awesome, regenerative powers that we all possess *when wrongly approached and utilized,* i.e. when not in accordance with the True Will; and indeed a great degree of self-knowledge is required before one can safely employ these forces.

---

[13] Crowley, A. (1983). *The Equinox*, Vol. III, No. 9. York Beach, ME: Weiser, 97–8.

From a Judeo-Christian perspective, these so-called "evil" forces can be seen as being roughly equivalent to the *nephesh* in our Qabalistic psychology model—the vital force or "animal soul." Judeo-Christian orthodoxy would see this as the supposedly evil natural drives and impulses, the sexual force, aggressive vitality, and so on. In contrast, our Thelemic perspective understands the *nephesh* is just as divine as all other created things. It is life-giving, generative power—our task is to understand the right time to tap into it during our initiatory journey. We first forge a strong link to the *neshamah* and the HGA, before endeavoring to engage intensely with the forces residing in the *nephesh*.

So, while the traditional Judeo-Christian view of these primal forces casts them in a negative light, our Thelemic understanding is quite different. There are even some important clues to be unlocked with *gematria*. The Hebrew words for serpent (*nachash*) and messiah (*mashiach*) both enumerate to 358, so we have an implied equivalence between the serpent and the redeemer. The number 358 also includes encoded relationships between the numbers 3, 5, and 8, which in turn relate to the pentagram, and therefore also to the life force, or *kundalini*. Rightly understood, the serpentine *nephesh*—the very thing that society has condemned as evil for millennia—is itself our redeemer; but we must approach it with an initiated understanding of its nature, and put it to use in line with our conscious intention and True Will. This initiated understanding begins with thorough work with our own shadow, so let's review some tools that may be useful for this.

We would not likely tell a preadolescent child to work on their shadow-stuff, because they don't even know who they are yet. For the most part, an adolescent is just beginning to get their ego/*ruach* figured out. What are they like as a person? What are their values? What early glimmerings of True Will are beginning to speak to them? It would not be wise to tell someone at that stage of development to forget about finding themselves, and simply dive into the morass of shadow-shit; but this is exactly what we are in danger of doing along our initiatory path if we set aside the pursuit of the K&C of the HGA in favor of playtime with demons. It's not evil, it's not wrong *per se*, but it sure as hell could be *distracting*, and delay an initiate's deeper apprehension of their True Will. We must go through a "spiritual adolescence" to attain K&C, before moving on to this shadow work. You may be aware that in the system of Abramelin, the magician first attains the K&C of their HGA, and *only then* binds the four "princes of evil" to their Will and the service of the HGA. It is this conscious link to *neshamah* that fully enables us to rightly understand and utilize the primal forces of the *nephesh*; that is, to ensure that our drives and impulses are put in service to the True Will rather than being allowed to dictate our decisions and actions reactively and unwisely.

In the system of A∴A∴, long before K&C, we see the Neophyte beginning their work with the *nephesh*. This includes their work with the 32nd path of Tav, where the task is to attain mastery of the Body of Light, or astral/energetic body. The Neophyte strengthens their ability to scry the astral worlds through astral projection and similar techniques. The final formal test of this capacity involves scrying the *qlippoth* of their own natal sun sign—definitely a magical form of "shadow work."

Aside from formal work in a magical order, I encourage all aspirants to engage in shadow work on a purely psychological level via dream analysis, psychotherapy, and monitoring of psychological projections. Robert Johnson's *Inner Work*[14] and Soror Meral's various writings on projections are my perennial recommendations for this, but I'd like to draw your attention to another long-time favorite of mine, Robert Moore and Douglas Gillette's *King, Warrior, Magician, Lover.*[15] In the original text, Moore and Gillette present these as archetypes of masculinity, but I think there are broader lessons to draw from the material. They discuss the Magician archetype as the possessor of immense and secret power—power that goes

---

[14] Johnson, R. (1986). *Inner Work*. San Francisco: HarperSanFrancisco.

[15] Moore, R., & Gillette, D. (1990). *King, Warrior, Magician, Lover: Rediscovering the Archetypes of the Mature Masculine*. San Francisco: HarperOne.

beyond the understanding of mainstream culture and science—which involves the use of lesser-known forces requiring specialized knowledge and practices. A magician in their "fullness," in my view, is engaged in the right use of this secret power in accordance with True Will. The shadow side of the Magician archetype, in contrast, involves the misuse of this power, typically for mere ego-driven ends, ignorant of True Will. This is pretty much Crowley's definition of black magick (I'm looking at you, Klingsor[16]). This shadow-magician energy could manifest in blind aggression, detached manipulation of others (a waste of energy at best), tyranny, and oppression of others.

Many of us, when we first approached magick, were very likely on some sort of power trip, consciously or not. The ego all too easily turns to aggressive control tactics when it feels insecure, and insecurity is one of the ego's most common characteristics. In our drive for safety and dominance, we ignore our shadow material, and it becomes more likely for us to fall into it. The remedy for this, in addition to psychological self-discovery on its own plane, is to strive toward the HGA and the True Will, and then to align ourselves in every thought, word, and deed with enacting that Will, inwardly as well as in our work in the outer world. When a magician lives like this, real evil can never thrive within them. This is truly a magician in their fullness.

---

[16] See *Parsifal*, where the wizard Klingsor is portrayed as a power-mad, insecure, possessive tyrant—a fitting symbol of the misguided magician's ego, to be sure.

CHAPTER 4

SATURN AND JUPITER IN THE LIFE OF A THELEMITE

Part One: Saturn—Thinking Inside the Box

Every human being is inevitably beset with occasional phases of spiritual and emotional heaviness, restrictions, and hard lessons learned. If you have any familiarity with astrological symbolism, these statements likely call to mind the nature of the planet Saturn. In this section of the chapter, I'll discuss the symbolism of Saturn, drawn from mythology, astrology, and Qabalah, and then give suggestions about how we can work *with* its energies, not against them, to foster our own growth. When this Saturnian heaviness hits us, what can we do about it, and how do we *actively* learn from it?

The planet Saturn, astrologically and Qabalistically, is viewed as the bringer of form and structure, and the teacher of life lessons. You may have heard of the astrological "Saturn return," in which (approximately every twenty-nine and a half years) the planet returns to its position as it was on a person's natal chart. Astrologers tend to regard the Saturn return as a major time of life restructuring: If something is out of whack in your life, in an inner or outer sense, Saturn will tend to knock it right back in. This is rarely comfortable!

We can see Saturn as a mixed bag of intense, restrictive enforcement of form and severity in one's life; but this does *not* have to be a bad thing, if you approach it mindfully and explore the lessons it may teach. We've all heard the phrase "thinking outside the box" in reference to those times when, to get past a creative impasse or some other obstacle in life, the solution is to get out of the "box" of our restricted vision, closed-mindedness, or limiting habits. (We'll deal with that in the next part of this chapter, on Jupiter.) In contrast, our task here is to think *inside* the box, consciously striving to accept and learn from the restrictions that appear to bind us.

In ancient mythology, Saturn was a titan, and the Romanized name for Chronos in the original Greek pantheon. The Titans were the parents of the gods, and were themselves the children of Gaia and Uranus. (You know you're dealing with an ancient mythology when the gods have grandparents.) One way that Chronos, who we also know as "Father Time," restricts us is in the Saturnian enforcement of a *timeline* on our existence. We live in a finite world, only having a certain amount of freedom before death claims us. (Saturn, like the Grim Reaper, is often pictured with a scythe.) Our human bodies *must* live within the bounds of time.

On the Qabalistic Tree of Life, Saturn shows up in a couple of places, one of which is the third sephira, called Binah. The symbolism of Binah includes that of the Great Mother, the archetypal sea, and the womb of all creation that gives *form* to *force*. This is worth pondering. If you have an impulse to do something, but you're not sure exactly how to do it, you have force but no *context* (i.e., form) for its application. The form-giving, and therefore restrictive, nature of Saturn gives us this context in all of life, just as the limitations of time give deeper meaning to what you do with your life. This is one way we can see Binah as the "womb of creation"—Chokmah ("wisdom") is given context by Binah ("understanding"). We *must* have this "box" or form to contain the energies of life in order for them to truly exist.

Another important symbol of Binah is the archetypal Grail. In Thelemic cosmology, this is often seen as the cup of Babalon, but as a basic symbol, the Grail is simply a receptacle that gives form, just as *any* cup gives form to the liquid it contains. This containment is one expression of Saturnian restriction in the sense that the liquid can't flow anywhere; it is bound by the specific form of the cup. Yet, this restriction is often the very thing that enables us to interact efficiently with the world within us and around us. Licking wine off the floor doesn't work as well as drinking it from a cup. (If you don't believe me, test it yourself with your friends. Their amusement will be directly proportional to the amount of wine you've already consumed.) Party tricks aside, we can see that the cup restricts the liquid in the same way that life and its constraints force our minds, bodies, and energies into a certain form—a form we can't escape from, but which actually *enables* us to live and act effectively.

The Saturnian Grail is also seen as the Holy of Holies, the shrine above the Abyss—a place of transpersonal reality, where we move beyond the restrictions of the individual ego and personality; a place that is deeper, more ancient, and more true than anything that *could* exist in our personal lives and our everyday awareness. The crossing of the Abyss, and the attainment of the corresponding cosmic consciousness, is of course the work of the Master of the Temple—the Magister Templi grade of A∴A∴.

Consider these facts in light of geometry. The first supernal sephira is Kether, the dimensionless point at the root of all manifestation. The second sephira is Chokmah, and with this second "point" we can draw a line—the geometrical expression of the concept of force and direction, representing the first dimension. But without a third point—that is, without context for the force—there can be no form, and Binah/Saturn is that third point. This allows us to create a triangle, the simplest two-dimensional form, which in turn explains the prominence of the "trinity" in various cosmologies and creation myths. Thus, geometrically and philosophically, Saturn/Binah actually *embodies* the underlying concept it represents. It is the most basic form that can show us what form even *is*.

Saturn corresponds to the *muladhara* chakra, which is at the root of the spine and represents survival mechanisms and related instinctual drives. Other traditional correspondences of Saturn include the opium poppy, the metal lead, the color black, and the incense myrrh. It is also the archetypal *yoni* of tantric philosophy, which unites with the *lingam* in the cosmic sexual act of creation. The so-called "magical power" of Binah is described as the Vision of Sorrow and the Vision of Wonder, a pairing which should not surprise us, for so often our wonderment at the mysteries of life can only fully emerge once we have experienced its sorrows.

Let's look at some of the ways Saturn plays itself out in our practical lives. Legendary musician and producer Brian Eno has often spoken about the value of limitation in the creative process. He sees that when we purposely restrict ourselves, we can unleash a certain brand of creativity and novel thinking that would not otherwise have been available to us. Let's say I want to write a poem. I could simply write any words, in any order, on any place on the page. Alternatively, I might decide to impose a structure on the poem, such as restraining it to contain only ten lines, or to be in iambic pentameter. This sort of restriction unleashes a certain form of creativity that forces me to think in a special way, "inside the box," if you will, and might just result in a poem that is more beautiful than it would have been without those rules. Similarly, a musician has to work within the limitations of the instrument. You can't play a guitar by blowing on it, but you can play a flute pretty well that way. It is the limitations of an instrument that actually make the instrument *what it is*. In visual art, this might include the limitations of the color palette or the medium.

Another practical expression of Saturn is the act of *concentration*. In order to concentrate on something, you must restrict your focus. To accomplish anything in life, you must maintain focus on that thing long enough to follow through with doing it. (Theoretically, maintaining focus on any desired outcome long enough necessitates that it actually occurs, but of course, in most of life, great patience and persistence are required for larger aims to be realized.) Sustained attention on any action is therefore essentially meditation—the Saturnian process of narrowing and restricting our focus in order to get something accomplished. This might involve a stilling of the mind as in formal meditation, or it might express itself as a creative process where we purposely restrict ourselves to a task or timeline, as in "I'm going to sit down for two hours every day and work on this book!" Here again, creative and constructive action is potentiated by restriction. To give a simpler everyday example, if I want to pick up and drink a glass of water, some part of my brain has to stay focused on that task long enough for me to reach out, grab it, and drink it. If I lose that focus, I'll just be sitting and staring at it.

How do we as humans respond to restriction as we conventionally perceive it? How do we deal with Saturn in adaptive or maladaptive ways when we are struggling? At the personality level, we often experience it as sadness, heaviness, frustration, or stagnation. Most of us don't enjoy being limited—it tends to really piss off the ego. So what do we do when we feel that way? Often, we try to escape somehow. This might manifest in abandonment: "Screw this, I'm giving up." It could also manifest through addiction, feeding the desire to numb the pain of restriction and its harsh lessons by just zoning out. When we feel vulnerable, scared, or trapped, and Saturn is bearing down on us, we may also be more tempted to depend unhealthily on others, to envelop ourselves in the simplistic certainty of groupthink, or to lash out like a cornered animal.

Let's return to the concept of time for a moment. Earlier, we discussed Chronos, the personification of chronological time. But there is another kind of time in Greek language and philosophy: It's called *kairos*, or sacred time. When is it the right time to propose marriage to your beloved—is it 6:07 p.m., or 6:08 p.m.? There is no "right" chronological time, of course, but there is a right *sacred* time—that moment when the energy is just right, you're feeling connected to each other, and you simply know the time is *now*. Likewise, to bring it back to the creative process, if we are writing a song, we can't just say to ourselves, "At 8:16 p.m. I'll complete the second verse." That would be nice, but it doesn't work that way. We have to follow the creative impulse when it strikes. This is why true creative acts are *always* in tune with the world of the sacred. So, in life generally, when *chronos* is oppressing us, "softening" our attitude into one of receptive expectation of the right thing happening at the right time can be a key coping tool.

The late Robert Johnson was one of my favorite Jungian authors and speakers. He often lectured on the task of allowing the Spirit to enter into our daily lives, and one of his primary examples involves *paradox*. Paradox has a relationship to Saturnian restriction in that it creates confusion. We can't make sense of things or figure out what the right choice is through conventional means, so some other part of us has to activate. This is a recipe for novel and creative thinking. We must embrace the stuckness, work through the stagnation and frustration, and trust that it will bring us across the threshold to some new awareness if we can keep our focus.

Let's return to Brian Eno for another practical tip on those stuck points in life. In the 1970s, in keeping with his thesis that restriction and limitation can bring creative breakthroughs, Eno created the Oblique Strategies cards:[17] a set of small cards, each with one command written on it. If he got to a stuck place in the recording studio and a song wasn't going anywhere, he would draw a card and make himself do whatever it said, thus imposing a voluntary restriction on the process. Imagine yourself in a really stuck and frustrated place. Wouldn't it be nice to draw one of these cards and *make yourself* do whatever it says, trusting that it would at the very least present a definite playing field within which you might determine a course of action? Examples of the commands include things like "Ask people to work against their better judgment" and "Use unqualified people." Eno took such suggestions quite literally in his album *Taking Tiger Mountain (By Strategy)*,[18] where he utilized an orchestra composed of people who were barely trained to play their instruments! Other examples include "Only one element of each kind" and, my personal favorite, "Make a sudden destructive unpredictable action. Incorporate." One could undertake a rather humorous thought experiment by imagining the various life scenarios in which this last strategy might be employed . . . although I wouldn't recommend it while driving a car or operating heavy machinery.

On a more serious note, in terms of practical tools, I hope that if you haven't already done so you will commit to some sort of ongoing meditation practice. This training of the mental and spiritual muscles involved in holding our attention steady and stilling ourselves gets us out of the perpetual clatter of the human mind and the crazy society we live in. It allows a voice to speak within us that is usually drowned out by all this noise. By holding ourselves in this way to such a seemingly restrictive and limiting practice, we in fact *expand* our freedom to think and act in accordance with True Will, and to attain the goals we set for ourselves.

One final psychological tool: practice the "radical acceptance" of all reality. After all, you only have two choices at any given moment: accept what is happening to you, or don't accept what is happening to you. You'll notice that regardless of your choice, *it's still happening to you.* Therefore, it's best to work with it and not deny it. We must accept that, as unlikeable, untenable, oppressive, and wretched as our present situation may be, the starting place for making it better is completely accepting the experience being offered to us. In Thelemic terminology, we would call this worship of Nuit,[19] the goddess of all possibilities and realities. This is perhaps the ultimate instruction of Saturn. Only by accepting everything presented to us, and by truly thinking *inside that box*, can we find our way out of it.

Part Two: Jupiter—Breaking Out of the Box

As we discussed in the previous section, Saturn is emblematic of the often uncomfortable, yet instructive, restrictions and limitations of life. Jupiter,

---

[17] Available at *https://www.enoshop.co.uk/shop.*

[18] Eno, B. (1974). *Taking Tiger Mountain (By Strategy).* Island Records.

[19] See Chapter 7 of the present volume.

in contrast, embodies the expansiveness that eternally pushes back against those restrictions. In this section, we'll review these concepts on a psychological level as well as in relation to the path of Adepthood, and I'll suggest a few practical approaches to invoking and harnessing Jupiter's power in your life.

Consciously or not, most of us are constantly trying to balance the tension between Saturn and Jupiter—between restriction and expansion, restraint and impulsivity, order and spontaneity—in our lives. We need to have enough order and structure to frame our daily lives and give us space to work efficiently, but we shouldn't let that stifle our creativity, or inhibit our joy in discovering new mysteries and questing after new levels of consciousness or life experiences. If we simply accepted *all* the restrictions that Saturn places upon us, we wouldn't grow very much. On the other hand, if we *never* settled for the restrictions that Saturn places upon us, we also wouldn't grow very much. The dynamic balance between Saturn and Jupiter is the very heartbeat of life itself.

On the Tree of Life, we find Jupiter attributed to the sephira Chesed. Mythologically it's associated with Zeus, the so-called king of the gods, and we can understand its psycho-spiritual role as that of the Demiurge of Gnostic philosophy. Joseph Campbell once supposedly commented, "The problem with Jehovah is that he thinks he's God!" While the veracity of the quote is not well documented, it nevertheless speaks to the fact that Chesed/Jupiter is the highest conception of any "god" that is possible for the *ruach*. The various mythological conceptions of gods, including the monotheistic Judeo-Christian daddy-god in the heavens, are limited to the *ruach*'s tool set, whereas the transrational truth of the matter (i.e., in the supernal realm) is beyond human conception. *Any* images, myths, or qualities we project onto such gods are simply our own imaginings and are, at best, veils over this underlying truth.

All of this fits with Chesed's placement on the path of Adepthood. In our ascent up the Tree of Life, we have balanced the elemental realms below Tiphareth, and we have attained K&C at Tiphareth. In Geburah, we have focused and restructured our lives to honor our new and more complete awareness of True Will. Finally, we bring this process to full fruition in the Adeptus Exemptus grade of Chesed, signifying a completion of the archetype of human consciousness itself. This is the most any individual can evolve their own human consciousness at a personal (as opposed to a transpersonal) level. Just as the fully evolved *ruach* is our best vision of what a human can be in their fullness, so is the god-image of Chesed a human mind's best, but inevitably inadequate, shot at understanding what divinity truly is.

So how does Jupiter-consciousness manifest in everyday life? When life seems to bring us everything we need to be comfortable, to do our Will, and to perform our own distinctive Great Work, Jupiter is providing for us. It can bring us the "ease of circumstances" to perform the Great Work, as Crowley once put it.[20] In pop psychology parlance, we might call it an "attitude of abundance" rather than one of scarcity. When we indulge ourselves in mindful enjoyment of pleasure, not restricting or restraining ourselves, we embody Jupiter's nature. This essentially tantric "worship of Nuit'" occurs when we embrace the ecstasies available to us in everyday life, appreciating both the quantity and the quality of the things around us. Jupiter is also with us when we undertake anything that enhances the expansiveness of the self, such as negotiating for a raise to ensure we have all the resources we need, or moving into a new, larger home in order to have the space to spread ourselves out and indulge in our interests. Jupiter also includes the idea of positive occurrences that come to us unbidden, not just when we seek them out, and this explains the traditional association of Jupiter with "good luck."

Let's review some methods of invoking Jupiter. (Similar techniques could be used to invoke Saturn/Binah, or any other sephirothic, elemental, planetary, or zodiacal forces. See the "Methods of Ritual Construction" chapter of *Living Thelema* for much more on this.) As with any targeted invocation, there are a lot of options—and developing invocations and rituals that are powerfully and uniquely connected to us as

---

[20] Crowley, A. (1986). *De Arte Magica*. Seattle: Sure Fire Press.

individuals, and to the particular things we're trying to change in ourselves or our circumstances, is one of the most fun and creative aspects of being a magician. One example of a ritual for invoking Jupiter was presented in the *Living Thelema* chapter referenced just above, but with any formally structured ritual of this type, there will generally be preliminaries such as banishings, purifications, and consecrations, followed by some sort of general invocation, and then the specific invocations aimed at the ritual goal. Examples of these might include the Greater Hexagram Ritual of Jupiter, an invocation of the Jupiter Senior from an Enochian tablet, poetic invocations, or a reading of the chapter of *Liber VII*[21] attributed to Jupiter (Chapter III). In any case, you'll want to build in a way to carry the benefits of the ritual with you after it is completed. This might involve constructing a talisman of Jupiter to keep on your person, charging and consuming a eucharist of some sort, or creating a work of art while in the invoked "atmosphere." You could also simply perform a scrying of these astral regions and see what new awareness or information it brings.

A completely different approach would be to create a set of devotional practices keyed to Jupiter. There is overlap with a formal ritual approach, of course, since both would likely involve invocatory statements, but you can utilize the suggestions in Crowley's *Liber Astarte*[22] to flesh out the experience. For example, you could dedicate yourself to the god Zeus for an extended period of time, spending days, weeks, or even months performing daily devotional work.

Now let's review some practical, non-ritualized ways to enhance the Jupiterian quality in your life. I've already mentioned mindfulness of abundance and pleasure as one of these techniques. In saying "Will" at meals, you are mindfully eating and appreciating the quality of the food, as well as appreciating the enjoyment of the food. You can apply this principle to

---

[21] In Crowley, A. (1983). *The Holy Books of Thelema*. York Beach, ME: Red Wheel/Weiser.

[22] In Crowley, A. (1997). *Magick: Liber ABA* (2nd rev. ed.). Hymenaeus Beta (Ed.). York Beach, ME: Red Wheel/Weiser, LLC.

any other act in which you find engagement, pleasure, and focus: for example, walking through a forest and appreciating the texture of the leaves, the feeling of the ground under your feet, and the smell of the greenery. Any time you expand your awareness of these sensory inputs, and the richness and abundance of life, you are reveling in Jupiter's presence.

Conclusion

I have often suggested to my magical students, as well as my therapy clients, that there are two primary ways of finding intensity in life. One is the method of Jupiter: Turn up the volume! Live without restriction! Make everything bigger, louder, and . . . well . . . just *more*! The advantage of this approach is that it's generally fun and easy. However, we can't live this way all the time. Modern culture is full of examples of those who have burned out from such a lifestyle. Furthermore, human society itself seems to have been on a Jupiterian, expansive trajectory for more than a century now, and we can see the signs of the resulting strain in our climate, our addiction to technology, and our various materialistic obsessions. This suggests a second way of finding intensity in life, which is the method of Saturn: Listen more carefully! Be mindful of subtlety and fine detail. Train yourself in the Saturnian act of concentration, thereby constraining your attention and focus, so that you may perceive the intricacies of the *quietly intense* spaces in your outer and inner life.

I encourage you to think creatively about other ways to apply the principles discussed in this chapter to your life, so that you may find a point of peace in the delicate balance of expansive Jupiter and contracting Saturn. To paraphrase Crowley's statements in *Liber CLVIII*, "The Soldier and the Hunchback,"[23] the key is living not solely in the extremes of the pendulum's swing, but rather abiding in the stillness of the point from which the pendulum hangs.

---

[23] In Crowley, A. (1993). *The Equinox*, Vol. I, No. 1. York Beach, ME: Weiser.

CHAPTER 5

THE ORDEALS OF
THE GRADES OF A∴A∴

I've been studying and working the path of A∴A∴, as a student and a teacher, for more than thirty years now. While the specific manifestations of the triumphs and pitfalls of the Great Work are always somewhat unique to each individual aspirant, it is also the case that we can predict general trends in the initiate's evolution which are keyed to the grades of the order themselves. In this chapter, we'll review these landmarks of an aspirant's development as they move through the grades. Our discussion will apply most explicitly to someone formally working path of A∴A∴, but it may be useful as well to non-initiates who find themselves challenged by the ordeals of life itself. For example, the ordeals of Malkuth tend to relate to the physical world and the physical body, and our work in these realms may be most pronounced when we are formally working the Neophyte grade. Yet we are never without a physical body, we never live apart from the physical world, and we must always seek health and balance in this regard, no matter our initiatory grade or lack thereof.

There is a great deal of written instructional material in the system of A∴A∴ that can give us strong hints about what these ordeals are, but our focus here will be on the oaths and tasks of the grades themselves. Specifically, we'll look at the aspects of tasks that bind us to a particular endeavor—not just practicing a particular ritual or memorizing a Holy Book. We'll concentrate on those parts of the oaths and tasks that bind us to a certain way of living, or to a specific path of inner exploration. Whenever we take a magical oath we hold to be sacred, we enter into a binding commitment to the universe that we will uphold it. Even if you take a purely psychological point of view on the nature of oaths and the universal energies that enforce them (which, by the way, I do not), it would seem clear that *some part of you*, consciously or not, will punish you if you don't live up to that promise. *Something in you* will judge you for your failure, and this alone is harsh enough to inflict a good deal of pain. All aspirants should approach the oaths and grades of A∴A∴, or other any magical order, with full understanding that the work *will transform you* even if you later decide not to cooperate. I recall a particular Neophyte who expressed surprise in my belief that his ongoing ordeals were possibly related to his grade. Why in the hell would someone undertake this work with the expectation that it would *not* be so? Why would they sign up for a course of magical training if they believed it to be so ineffectual at having a transformative effect on their life?

Probationer

Every oath describes the work of the grade rather literally—the aspirant promises to prosecute the Great Work as relevant to their particular stage of training. In the oath of the Probationer, we read that their work is "to obtain a scientific knowledge of the nature and powers of my own being."[24] And in the task of the Probationer, we read that "they shall perform any tasks that the A∴A∴ may see fit to lay upon them. Let them be mindful that the word Probationer is no idle term, but that the Brothers will in many a subtle way *prove* them when they knoweth it not." Importantly, statements such as these give us clues about each grade's distinctive

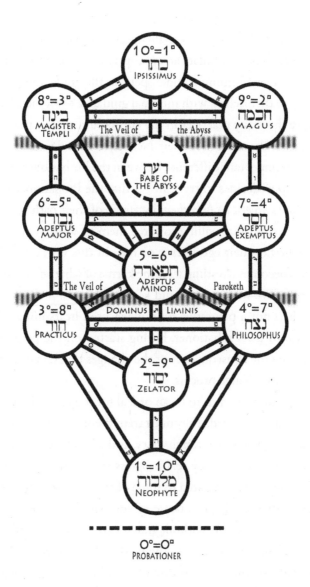

ordeals. In a fundamental sense, ordeals come when we tackle the grade tasks, presenting us with an opportunity to grow through them and actually dig into the work. Ordeals are like the helpful (but unpleasant) feedback we get from a physical injury, as the pain shows us where healing is needed. In the inner work of the grades, when we feel ourselves bumping up against an ordeal, obstacle, or challenge, we are forced to take a look at it and (if we are wise) formulate an appropriate course for growth.

In the one-year (minimum) time spent in the grade, the Probationer is left mostly to themselves, with minimal guidance from their Neophyte. They sample the many practices in the curriculum as they prefer, setting something of a "baseline" for their Neophyte to judge future training needs; but the important difference between the Probationer and a magician who simply "decides to try stuff" is that the Probationer has essentially *asked the universe to help them* by virtue of their oath. Once asked, the universe seems quite willing to force them to walk the path and do the work, whether their ego likes it or not. In this way, one of the primary ordeals becomes wrestling with the karma of what you have brought onto yourself. (We must understand karma as the amoral laws of cause and effect. It is not a pejorative term when used in its initiated sense.) So the ordeal of the Probationer, having started on the path, is largely about accepting the consequences of the changes that come about when we commit to *any* change process.

Self-discipline also tends to be an ordeal for the Probationer, because the grade is so unstructured. They must train themselves to sit down every day, do the work, keep a thorough diary, and actually "get with the program" if they are to make any real progress at all. This may sound simple—a minor obstacle compared to some of the more advanced practices of meditation or magick—but those of you who have tried to commit yourself to a path like this without much externally imposed structure know the challenges it can bring. The work of the Probationer is a confrontation with the rigors of self-discipline, and is indeed a "proving" of them, in the sense that it involves much necessary testing and preparation.

Let me offer a personal example. During my Probation, I found myself rather suddenly and unexpectedly having a terrible work experience. I was

---

[24] All quotations in this chapter involving oath or task papers are drawn from *Liber CLXXXV* (*Liber Collegii Sancti*), which is the name given to all of these grade papers collectively.

still living in Indiana, and really not feeling a good fit with anything I was doing after emerging from my graduate program in clinical psychology. It felt truly horrible at the time, but it was largely the aversiveness of that experience that forced me out to California and into the backyard of Soror Meral—a move that put me directly on track to discover and carry out my True Will. These experiences can be painful or upsetting at the time, but the whole point is to begin to decode how, whether they are perceived as positive or negative by the ego, they are shaping us to be stronger vessels for the light of the HGA, and better prepared therefore to execute our own Great Work. This applies to the ordeals of every grade, of course, but Probationers do seem to receive an especially intense dose of it.

Neophyte

In the oath of the Neophyte, we read that their work is "to obtain control of the nature and powers of my being, to observe zeal and service to the Probationers under me and to deny myself utterly on their behalf." It doesn't get much plainer than that. The Neophyte is bound to service by oath. Among other things, this is an ego ordeal, because if a Neophyte continues to hold on to the idea that the main purpose of progress on the spiritual path is for their own personal benefit rather than to be of service to those who come after, it can cause an awful lot of problems. In my experience, the further one goes believing that, the greater the intensity of the problems that arise—"the bigger they are, the harder they fall" seems an apt summary. We see this reach a pinnacle of ugliness at the Adeptus Exemptus grade with the so-called "Black Brothers" clinging to magical power and personal attainment as if this were the main point. It is here at the Neophyte grade, however, that the initiate is first forced, by the strength of their own oath, to commit to a life of service. In fact, one of the primary practical tasks of the Neophyte is to undertake the work of the path of Tav connecting Malkuth and Yesod, and this path is itself sometimes referred to as the Path of Service.

The task of the Neophyte mandates that "he shall perform any tasks that his Zelator in the name of the A∴A∴ and by its authority may see fit to lay upon him. Let him be mindful that the word Neophyte is no idle term, but that in many a subtle way the new nature will stir within him, when he knoweth it not." A similar statement was presented in the oath of the Probationer, and in both these cases, this largely relates to the tasks of initiated life itself. Yet, in the case of the Neophyte, there may also be tasks specifically assigned by the supervising Zelator. So why is the word Neophyte "no idle term"? This is a clue about the ordeal and the growth process as well. The English word Neophyte originates from the Greek *neophytos*, "newly planted." What do we know about a newly planted seed? We know that it begins to express its basic nature and innate growth patterns, and to take on the outward characteristics of the mature plant it is to become. When the Neophyte of A∴A∴ begins their journey their basic nature (that is, their True Will) is mostly unconscious, and its emergence can be surprising, shocking, or even frightening. It may not have much to do with the way in which they have previously thought of themselves—they may not be growing into the person they expected! Staying with our plant metaphor: If they were expecting to be an orange tree, they may find themselves to be an oak instead. An ordeal of the Neophyte is thus to begin to come to terms with their basic nature as it starts to outwardly express itself. In this grade, the stirrings of True Will begin to take shape and demand outward expression in a way that is aligned with our magical oaths.

We also read in the task of the Neophyte that "he shall in every way fortify his body." This is what newly planted seeds need as well: the proper conditions for growth, suited to the type of seed in question. So as Neophytes, we have to figure out what we need physically, but we are also nurturing the True Will. That is, we must determine the conditions best suited to the Will, so we can reshape our outer lives to be aligned with our growth process. This may require a change in relationships, jobs, or geographic locations, or there may be other, more subtle things that need realignment. Psychologically speaking, we must balance our inner temperament by facing the four tests the task paper refers to as the "Powers of the Sphinx": Knowledge, Will, Courage, and Silence. Each of these Powers represents a certain attribute that needs to be nurtured, expressed, and balanced with the other three. As with many other ordeals, these are most often presented to us by life itself, but specific tests may be constructed by the Neophyte's supervising Zelator.

The ordeals of the Neophyte and beyond are referenced in Crowley's New Comment on *The Book of the Law*, Chapter 3, verse 64 (*AL* III:64): "Let him come through the first ordeal & it will be to him as silver." Crowley comments: "The four ordeals now to be described, represent the ascent of the aspirant from the tenth and lowest of these spheres, which refers to the earth, unregenerate and confused, in which the aspirant is born."[25] We have already discussed that the work of the Neophyte includes passage of the path of Tav, and an ordeal related to this passage has sometimes been referred to as the "ordeal of the *nephesh*." We can understand this as wrestling with unconscious material, drives and impulses that may distract us from the Great Work. In some places Crowley describes this as a literal temptation off the path by a "woman," but I encourage you not to take this too literally. If we consider the ordeal of the Neophyte in relation to the story of Parsifal, we will recall that Parsifal is bewitched by Kundry, who (along with the "flower maidens") is the emblem of pleasurable earthly distractions, Malkuth, and the final Heh of the Tetragrammaton, and in doing so he eventually comes to find Spirit in the physical world. Just so, the Neophyte must peer behind the veil of matter to detect the immanent Spirit therein; but they must also know what to *do* with it and how to exalt it. In the story, Parsifal takes Kundry to the Grail castle and she essentially *becomes* the Grail herself. (See Chapter 10 for more on this.) We experience ordeals of this sort when we fail to comprehend that Spirit interpenetrates all that we are and all that we do in the physical world. The path of Tav also includes intensive work with the Body of Light, or astral body, and this work itself tends to stir up the primal energies of the lower psyche (i.e., the *nephesh*). These energies are one way of understanding the nature of the "silver" referred to in the quote. It is no small matter to face these forces, integrating them into consciousness, and this is yet another ordeal of the Neophyte.

Zelator

Crowley's commentary on *AL* III:64 continues:

> *He riseth in the first ordeal to the sphere called the Foundation, numbered 9, and containing, among other ideas, those of the generative organs, air, the moon, and silver. Its secret truth is that stability is identical with change; of this we are reminded by the fact that any multiple of 9 has 9 for the sum of its digits.*
>
> *The initiate will now perceive that the sum of the motions of his mind is zero, while, below their moon-like phases and their Air-like divagations, the sex-consciousness abides untouched, the true foundation of the temple of his body, the root of the Tree of Life that grows from earth to heaven. This Book is now to him "as silver." He sees it pure, white and shining, the mirror of his own being that this ordeal has purged of its complexes. To reach this sphere he has had to pass through a path of darkness where the Four Elements seem to him to be the universe entire. For how should he know that they are no more that the last of the 22 segments of the Snake that is twined on the Tree?*
>
> *Assailed by gross phantoms of matter, unreal and unintelligible, his ordeal is of terror and darkness. He may pass only by*

---

[25] Crowley, A. (1991). *The Law Is for All*. Israel Regardie (Ed.). Phoenix: New Falcon Publications, 327.

favour of his own silent God, extended and exalted within him
by virtue of his conscious act in affronting the ordeal.[26]

The oath of the Zelator directs that they must "obtain control of the foundations" of their own being. The word "foundation" is of course the name of the sephira Yesod, as Crowley referenced in the quote above. The task adds, "He shall in every way establish perfect control of his automatic consciousness." Not unexpectedly, all of these are pointing toward the basic nature of Yesod. This is the realm of sexuality, generativity, and the personal unconscious. What are the ordeals associated with this grade? When we swear an oath to devote ourselves to perfect control of our automatic consciousness, we soon discover that it's a rather chaotic and murky place, with the winds of the mind blowing us about mercilessly—Yesod is the sphere of air, after all. We must attempt to find some sense of stability in that place of perpetual change. Being "assailed by phantoms of matter and the ordeals of terror and darkness" refers to grappling with our own hidden self, and attempting to harness the generative, life-giving forces that reside within it. We must embrace the primal power of *kundalini* within us and direct it, under Will, toward the higher aims of our work.

Any time we are dealing with ordeals involving this kind of uncertainty and identity-shaking, issues of dependency tend to arise. When we feel this unstable, we tend habitually and reactively to reach out to any available sources of support, guidance, or (most pathologically) anesthesia. So in the Zelator grade, it is fairly common to see issues of overdependence on people—the classic but clichéd "codependent" relationship. Also, substance dependency is not unlikely—anything that makes the fear and pain stop, even temporarily, will be at risk of overuse. The solution to this is to maintain vigilance in our conscious and willful persistence in confronting these fears. Monitoring our psychological projections (see the chapter on the role of the ego in the Great Work in *Living Thelema*) is one incredibly

---

[26] Ibid.

important tool for learning about these hidden corners of the psyche, as is psychotherapy, and in particular dreamwork, inasmuch as it deals directly with the realm of symbols, the natural language of the unconscious. Most repression or avoidance of unconscious material is a recipe for illness and imbalance, and this, if unchecked, can knock us off the path irretrievably.

Practicus

In the oath of the Practicus, we read that their work is "to obtain control of the vacillations" of their own being. In the task, the Practicus is directed to "in every way establish perfect control" of their wit. And of course, "wit" here is not referring to a sense of humor *per se*, but to the intellect overall. Both of these are clear indications that we are dealing with the sephira Hod. This is the sphere of the normal human intellect. In contrast to the Zelator, who endeavored to master those "air-like divinations" of the unconscious mind in its raw form, here the Practicus is faced with controlling the conscious elements of the mind and fine-tuning them. The tasks of this grade can be generally related to the path of Gnana Yoga, "union through knowledge"—we see extensive work with Qabalah, and the highly technical Enochian system of magick, for example.

The danger here, the ordeal if you will, is getting lost in the "swamp" of intellect. Thelemites tend to be pretty brainy types, and when one is in a stage of work that emphasizes intellectual faculties, this can be a real hazard. Any time you are on home turf, dealing with familiar and therefore probably comfortable aspects of self, there is a tendency to like it too much—to linger there, overemphasize it, and fail to move on to less charted regions. I have seen many initiates get bogged down in this way. They "think themselves" into circles, and get stuck. This is not always uncomfortable, necessarily. It sometimes involves simply settling in and becoming an "armchair magician" and really enjoying the hell out of that; but at some point we have to remember that there is action to be taken, and the fires of devotion we are approaching in Netzach need to be stoked. You won't have to look very far to find examples of these kinds of magicians who clearly spend more time theorizing, debating, and arguing than they do practicing. If you spend even ten minutes perusing Thelemic social media groups, you will find ample evidence for this assertion. Don't get stuck in the swamp!

Philosophus

The oath of the Philosophus states that initiates of this grade must "obtain control of the attractions and repulsions" of their being. The elemental grades of A∴A∴ can be mapped to the four Jungian functions, and Netzach connects most closely to the "feeling" function. This mode of consciousness is one of the "valuing" functions: It says, "This feels good. I want to get closer to it," or alternatively, "This feels bad. I want to get the hell away from it!" It tells us whether we love something or hate something, and this clearly connects to the oath's statement about the "attractions and repulsions" of our being. It is through the right use of the feeling function that we identify those things that are beautiful to us and deserving of devotion. This is how the Philosophus balances out the work of the lower spheres and comes face to face with the task of developing Right Devotion.

If we are overzealous in our use of this devotional tool, the feeling function, we put ourselves on a bit of a rollercoaster, emotionally speaking. We tend to have an attention deficit in the domain of loving things, and in order to really strengthen the muscles of devotion needed here, we must learn to *focus* our love and devotion in more precise ways. Conversely, if we *underutilize* the feeling function, then we are also hampered in our ability to aim it at any one chosen target. If we ignore this emotional, aspirational, and devotional side of ourselves, we are failing to use an incredibly important tool of spiritual progress. If we can't identify that which we love in a simple, day-to-day way, then how can we strive toward the Holy Guardian Angel with the necessary fervor and devotion? So, when we swear a sacred oath to control the attractions and repulsions of our being, we are promising to master our own ability to love and devote ourselves to anything we choose. The task statement makes it crystal clear: "They shall in every way establish perfect control of their devotion."

As we might expect when dealing with powerful emotions, the ordeals of the Philosophus can be understood in light of Netzach's attribution to the element of fire. Emotional regulation is a common problem, especially with regard to anger. Anger can be a fiery and intense thing, particularly for people who haven't done sufficient introspection (and perhaps a bit of psychotherapy) before reaching this grade; they may be blindsided by residual anger from childhood experiences or other unresolved situations in life. Accordingly, in my experience, dealing with anger management issues is probably the single most common psychological ordeal of the Philosophus.

Dominus Liminis

The oath of the Dominus Liminis indicates that the aspirant must "obtain control of the aspirations" of their being. It is easy to see how this follows from the Philosophus's attention to devotion—the muscles of devotion have been strengthened through their practice of *Liber Astarte* and other work—but initiates of this grade must actively utilize those muscles in continuous aspiration to the HGA. It is an intense process of focused devotion, and the pinnacle of Bhakti Yoga in the system of A∴A∴. Nearly every human being knows how to love something, and the Philosophus trains themselves to direct that love to a desired end. Now, the Dominus Liminis must learn how to hold their entire being in focused aspiration to the ONE worthy object—the HGA.

The task further states, "Besides all this, they shall abide upon the Threshold. Let them remember that the word Dominus Liminis is no idle term, but that their mastery will often be disputed, when they knoweth it not." The term itself means "Lord of the Threshold," and in the ordeal of this grade that is precisely the mastery that is "disputed." At this stage of the path, the initiate will inevitably be pushed around by the myriad forces of life that might tempt them to be distracted from the one goal of K&C, but they are oath-bound to strive to abide on that threshold of single-minded devotion and aspiration.

The task goes on to say, "They shall in every way establish perfect control of their intuition." That is, they must hold their focus, as described above, but determining precisely *where* to focus is largely an intuitive task. Intuition (to Jung) is a way of knowing truth that is completely independent of the physical senses. The Dominus Liminis must recognize their own most sacred truth without all of the outer evidence their intellect is accustomed to having; and the proper development of this ultimate truth-sense enables us to listen inwardly for, and accurately perceive, that one voice that is the HGA's, and discriminate it from all the others.

CHAPTER 6

CREATIVITY

W hen we are plugged into our deepest selves, thus having access to the divine power that resides there, we are most able to transmute that power into inspired, creative work. This chapter will discuss the relationship between the creative process and the path of magick and mysticism. Also, I'll give you some practical suggestions for enhancing your own creative work. In this discussion, I may use specific examples such as art or poetry, but it should be understood that what I say here will apply to any creative medium whatsoever, from art, music, and poetry to breakdancing and ballet. Even if you don't think of yourself as a creative artist in any of these media, my assertion is that the creative act is something we engage in every day as we live our lives. It is the translation of whatever is going on in our inner life into manifest results. The efficiency with which we can tap into that inner world, however we name or experience it, and turn it into tangible results in the outer world (whether in a creative form or just in our life itself) is, to a great extent, directly proportional to our level of inward initiation.

True art, in any medium, involves the transmutation of the ineffable into the manifest. Much like the path of initiation itself, in the early stages this is most often accomplished via the conscious mind being attentive to subconscious impulses toward creation. This might be a sudden flash of inspiration about an image, a poetic or musical phrase, a symbol, an innovative intellectual conception, and so on. Also, as we see with the initiate's intuition after attainment of K&C of the HGA, the creative person may find that there is a dramatic increase in the directness of their creative process. It is an increasingly *conscious* engagement with the superconscious or archetypal elements which fuel the creative work. Just as any adept might quite consciously perceive a directive from the HGA in some other avenue of life, so does the artist-adept perceive a clear imperative toward a particular creative expression. It often seems to me that for some great creative people, including William Blake and other venerated "saints" of our tradition, the voice of the HGA was in fact the source and seed of their creative output itself. In such cases, it didn't result in overtly magical or mystical work such as teaching in magical orders or producing holy books, but simply in divinely inspired creation manifesting in the world through their handiwork.

If you contemplate other great artists, musicians, or poets, I think you will find (much as Crowley seemed to feel) that the creative work itself, rightly understood and rightly executed, is inherently a divine and truly magical act. To put it in a different light, just as a magical ritual is best achieved by essentially "falling in love" with the object of the working, so too does creative expression require a certain ecstatic union with the artistic ideal. I should clarify that when I say "falling in love," I am not talking about "lust of result" or other egoic attachment to the object of the working. I'm talking about discovering that the magical goal is in line with our True Will. Some part of us—that part most deeply rooted in our Will—needs to fall in love with it, and we must pursue it with all our heart and might, and not just because it feels good to the ego. So, the artist is impelled to create out of a type of *love* for what they are trying to express. The artist is *entranced* with the process of engaging with the material. Indeed, they are compelled to do so—it seems a necessary step in life, every bit as much as eating or sleeping. The creative material that is coming through *wants* to be expressed, it seems, and we are the vessel of that expression. This is precisely analogous to the expression of the true and universal will through the totality of a human's life, when rightly and mindfully enacted.

Crowley comments on this general idea in Chapter 67 of *Liber Aleph*, "On the Poets." In the previous chapter, he has compared a poet to a Magus and so he is following up on that comparison in what he says here:

> For this Reason is the Poet called an Incarnation of the Zeitgeist, that is, of the Spirit or Will of his Period. So every Poet is also a Prophet, because when that which he sayeth is recognized as the Expression of their own Thought by Men, they translate this into Act, so that, in the Parlance of Folk vulgar, and ignorant, "that which he foretold is come to pass." Now then the Poet is Interpreter of the Hieroglyphs of the Hidden Will of Man in many a Matter, some light, some deep, as it may be given unto him to do. Moreover, it is not altogether in the Word of any Poem, but in the quintessential Flavor of the Poet, that thou mayest seek this Prophecy. And this is an Art most necessary to every Statesman. Who but Shelley foretold the Fall of Christianity, and the Organization of Labour, and the Freedom of Woman; who but Nietzsche declared the Principle at the Root of the World-War? See thou clearly then that in these Men were the Keys of the dark Gates of the Future; should not the Kings and their Ministers have taken heed thereto, fulfilling their Word without Conflict?[27]

Clearly, in Crowley's view, the creative person is a prophet not just of their own inspiration at the moment, but of humanity's evolution and its state of collective consciousness.

---

[27] Crowley, A. (1991). *Liber Aleph vel CXI: The Book of Wisdom or Folly.* York Beach, ME: Weiser, 67.

Another way of understanding the creative act is to relate it to the path of Daleth, the Empress. In the scheme of attributions drawn from the *Sepher Yetzirah*, which is sometimes called the Cube of Space, Daleth is attributed to the Eastern face of the Cube. This is the direction traditionally associated with the source of divine light, the dawning sun and so on. Daleth and the Empress are traditionally understood to relate to the power of creative imagination—the contemplation of divine forms, and the power that actually *expresses* divine forms. This constitutes the transmission or translation of creative impulses and forms across the Abyss into normal human consciousness, and thereby into the manifest world. In many ceremonial temples, such as those of the Hermetic Order of the Golden Dawn and its successors, the East is the place where the Hierophant and other Second Order members sit. These advanced members are especially charged with maintaining the so-called invisible stations and other "astral architecture" of the temple—the specific faculty of creative imagination under discussion here.

Consider also these correspondences from *777*[28] with reference to the fourteenth path of Daleth. Crowley gives success in Bhakti Yoga as the Hindu or Buddhist result attributed to Daleth. Likewise, the attribution of Aphrodite to this path connects the idea of creative work with a loving devotional process, as we were discussing earlier: "falling in love" with the object of the work. The animals attributed to Daleth are the dove—which calls to mind the descending dove on the O.T.O. lamen, representing the descending influx of divine power, among other things—and the swan. I encourage you to investigate the story of Parsifal, particularly Frater Achad's *The Chalice of Ecstasy*, in this light. The magical formula attributed to Daleth in *777* is Love. Seeing a theme develop here? Under suggestive correspondences, Crowley gives "the wife." In my view, this

---

[28] Crowley, A. (2005). *777 and Other Qabalistic Writings of Aleister Crowley*. York Beach, ME: Red Wheel/Weiser, LLC.

does not merely imply a female partner, but the much broader idea of the muse, the creative impulse itself, and the things onto which we project the source and goal of the creative impulse—the things that inspire us. We can read more on Daleth in Crowley's "The Two and Twenty Secret Instructions of the Master," where he writes:

> *This is the Harmony of the Universe, that Love unites the Will-*
> *to-create with the Understanding of that Creation: under-*
> *stand thou thine own Will!*

> *Love and let love! Rejoice in every shape of love, and get thy*
> *rapture and thy nourishment thereof!*[29]

Creation is, therefore, a *loving* act that bridges the individual mind with the supernal or transrational truth of the universe. It is the creative process of the universe itself, filtered through the eyes and hands of the particular human creator.

With all that as a theoretical foundation, let's talk about some practical considerations for enhancing creativity in your own life. Of course, there could be many different ways to approach this, but for our purposes here, I've broken it down into two general umbrella categories:

1. Loosening the rational mind's grip on moment to moment consciousness

2. Deepening the rational mind's access to transrational creative flow

So, if you need a concise mantra for this endeavor, I offer *loosening and deepening.*

Loosening may be fairly self-explanatory from what I have said already. We strive to loosen the habitual hold of the mental control that we tend to

---

[29] Crowley, A. (1992). *The Heart of the Master* (rev. ed.). Tempe, AZ: New Falcon Publications, 57.

cultivate as our normal state of consciousness. Our everyday ego-intellect wants things in categories and boxes. We want to predict what's coming and prepare for it. We want our lives to unfold according to conscious choices. Yet, none of these habits of thought are particularly conducive to creative work; on the contrary, they tend to dampen the flow of creative inspiration. This is partially because creative inspiration can actually feel *threatening* to the conscious mind. Creation is inherently chaotic in many ways, from the perspective of the ego, because it's unknown and constitutes a letting go of control.

What are some techniques for this loosening? Divination comes to mind. Whenever we intentionally turn to Tarot cards, I Ching sticks, or similar methods, we are practicing the art of letting go just a little bit; letting go of conscious control, or of outcomes or judgments. Astral projection and scrying are other places where loosening can happen. One of the barriers to successful astral projection is that clinging connection to the everyday rational mind and the physical body. People hit a wall with these practices largely because they require us to loosen our mental control from our habitual way of operating. Similarly, scrying forces us to defocus from outward sensory reality a just a bit and perceive what is coming through in the shewstone, mirror, or whatever medium we are using. Another loosening tool is letting some decisions be made by chance. For example, if you are faced with a binary choice— yes or no, left or right, Thai or pizza—you can flip a coin and purposely relinquish conscious control. The value in this is in the *practice* element, obviously, not in the import of the decisions themselves.

Another thing you can do is draw up a list of ten or fifteen relatively inconsequential rules for any given day, along the lines of "Today I will turn left when given the opportunity," or "Today I will avoid expressing an opinion about anything whatsoever." Select one or more of these rules at random each day—the random aspect is important—and vigilantly abide by them by as unbreakable commandments. The key is that we abdicate conscious decision making on a certain matter, and the matter *itself* is not necessarily of our own choosing. We are outsourcing some of the control to a randomization process.

Another loosening technique is to counter every thought with its opposite. Whenever you determine you have an opinion about something, purposely, silently, and inwardly argue with yourself. If you decide you don't like Joe, who sits in the cubicle next to you, immediately counter that with all the reasons that Joe is a great guy. Challenge your ego. Review the techniques Crowley describes in *Liber Os Abysmi*[30] for exhausting the rational mind in order to allow the transrational to break through. Full attainment in the practices of that liber would go far beyond our discussion here—this is a liber assigned to the Exempt Adept, after all—but you can pick and choose some of the techniques as useful thought experiments.

A final loosening technique, and probably the most "direct" of all those discussed here since it relates specifically to the creative act, is stream-of-consciousness writing, or similar improvisation in any creative medium. In other words, throw out the rule book and simply *play*. This is truly creative play in its purest sense: no rules, no limitations on creative possibilities, no time limits, no goals. Just sit down and write whatever comes to mind, or pick up a musical instrument and play whatever flows out of your fingers. Any time we open up to inspiration in this way, we train ourselves to be better at it in the future, and this tends to loosen the death grip of our conscious control over things.

Now, on to *deepening*. A useful framing image is that of digging a well into the subconscious mind. Eventually, we hit creative "water," and once that well is in place, the water tends to continue to flow—we don't have to re-dig the well over and over. This is exactly what we are doing with rigorous, sustained meditation practices, which are in fact my first suggested deepening technique. Keep up your daily work with *asana* (posture) and *dharana* (concentration) practices! (See *Living Thelema*

---

[30] In Crowley, A. (1993). *The Equinox*, Vol. I, No. 7. York Beach, ME: Weiser.

for basic guidelines.) A personal observation: I have found regular, deep meditation really is a magick formula for enhancing my musical creativity. When I keep up with it rigorously, *music just comes*. It's really much more like *finding* the music—or more accurately, the music finding me—rather than consciously creating it. I suspect you may find something similar with regard to your own preferred medium of creative expression. If you meditate regularly, those floodgates will tend to open. You may experience yourself as a channel and vessel for creation, and not merely as an intellectual "planner" or organizer of creative acts.

In the above example, I am referring to the style of meditation we might call "stilling," where the goal is to hold our focus on a particular image, mantra, or other object, restraining our mind from straying too away from it. An alternative approach involves "reflective" meditation. Here, we choose a word or phrase, a line from a holy book or other key text, and simply hold the word or phrase in mind as we are meditating. In contract with stilling meditation, we allow and even *encourage* associations to arise, without restraint or censorship. Simply follow the flow of your thought. Every few minutes, return to contemplation of the core phrase so that you are staying relatively close to it, rather than allowing the chain of associations to go on indefinitely. This functions as a deepening technique because when we repeatedly access this material—when we give our mind the space to let the ego get out of the way—that metaphorical "well" gets dug deeper and deeper. Such techniques can become one of the *primary* ways of learning things about ourselves and the universe. It's not rational, it's not planful, but it is *essential* to our inward initiatory progress that we learn how to extract information from sources other than our everyday human mind.

While each of us must ultimately find our own unique ways to unlock our creativity, I hope these practical suggestions will get you started!

CHAPTER 7

THE WORSHIP OF NUIT

As you likely know, Nuit is the name given in Thelemic cosmology to the star goddess who represents the totality of all existence. As Thelemites, we are urged to worship Nuit as one important aspect of our devotional practice. In this chapter, I am going to discuss one particular method of worshiping Nuit: the act of surrender. As it turns out, this process of surrender in its many forms can be a core theme in our worship, and in this discussion we are going to examine why this is the case.

I've been around the block a few times in Thelemic circles and I can predict, with a high degree of certainty, that the term *surrender* is unlikely to be a popular one for many Thelemites. It has a connotation of weakness, or perhaps a sense of giving over our will or our autonomy to someone or something; but bear with me, I'm going to use the term in a very specific manner that you may find less offensive!

Let's begin by reviewing some examples of this surrender. Consider physical pain. Think of the last time you had a bodily injury; perhaps you hurt your back or stubbed your toe. You will recall that wherever you are hurting there is a natural tendency to want to clench up around the pain, to tighten the muscles, to fight it, to force it to go away, or otherwise try to build some physical and psychic walls around it. Did you notice how much worse that made it? To reduce our experience of such pain, we must instead *soften* around it, not fight it, allowing it (hopefully) to dissipate naturally. This softening implies an acceptance. We thus *surrender* to the pain, and once accepted it can be transformed into a much less aversive experience. It actually hurts less, demanding less of our attention and allowing us to devote that attention to more constructive aims. Similarly, when our muscles are tense and in need of a stretch, the best way to stretch them further is not by holding on to the tension and fighting and pushing harder—we must instead relax and breathe. Try it now. Stand up and attempt to touch your toes. Now breathe and relax your muscles—you'll likely find you can stretch further than just a few moments earlier. Again, our acceptance and surrender to the stretching process is the key to enhancing it.

These physiological examples are, of course, also metaphors for an underlying psychological and spiritual process. One central method of worshiping Nuit is accepting the reality that is right in front of us—not pushing away *anything* we encounter in our everyday lives. We accept (i.e., surrender to) and adore all manifest experience as the aspect of Nuit we are currently being offered, it in spite of our ego-preferences to the contrary, which are so often present. Now, this acceptance of reality doesn't mean we cannot or should not attempt to shape our reality to be a better expression of our True Will or even our basic comfort, but we must accept the present moment as our starting place—much like how, when attempting to navigate using a map, if you don't accept where you are there is no way you are going to get where you want to go.

Another form of psychological surrender is letting go of fear and desire or "lust of result," which are absolutely ego-based. The real Self, the *neshamah*, the *khabs*-star at our center, doesn't feel fear and doesn't indulge in desire-based clinging to any particular life experience—it's beyond all of that. The ego is the part of us that clenches up, clings to things, runs away from things, fears things, and makes us feel like we won't be complete unless we have certain things. When we surrender the illusory control that the ego likes to think it has, we open ourselves up to our higher consciousness, allowing us to truly worship all existence (Nuit) *as we find it*. This is related to the process of crossing the Abyss, the formulas of LVX and NOX and the attainment of the Magister Templi grade of A∴A∴; it is the *willingness* to give up one's attainments and even one's sense of individual consciousness. We must be willing to acknowledge that all we have thought of as ourselves is but an illusion, as we offer it into the cup of our Lady Babalon, as an aspect of worship of Nuit. Even after K&C, the idea of being "an Adept with an HGA" can be a source of troublesome ego-pride.

Another extremely important form of surrender-as-worship is the surrender to mental uncertainty. The ego is a necessary perceptual organ we must use to efficiently interact with the outer world, and it mediates our inner experience with outer, practical realities. When the ego is kept in right relationship with the totality of ourselves, it functions just fine; but it's not always going to be able to find the solution to any given obstacle or problem. At some points, when faced with a dilemma or paradox, or a decision that seems insurmountable, the ego hits a wall. Maybe we're supposed to figure it out in the traditional sense, and we need to surrender to that reality of not knowing the answer. This surrender opens the door to the superconscious spiritual intuition of *neshamah*, a faculty of mind that is transrational and beyond egoic functioning. We are thereby guided to a very different but even more "real" answer to whatever dilemma we are facing—an answer which we could never have found through the efforts of the rational mind. So, paradoxically, sometimes admitting that we don't know, and indeed that we *can't* know, is exactly the step that brings the needed knowledge.

You may be asking yourself what all this talk of surrender has to do with the act of worship, and that is an understandable question. The simple answer is that spiritual ecstasy, the ecstasy that comes from union with Nuit, is more available to us when surrender is our firmly established mindset. Any pushing away of experience cuts us off from the ecstasy of union with that experience. And uniting passionately with any and every experience is precisely how we might define the worship of Nuit. The ecstasy of union with Nuit is embodied in the wonder and majesty available to us consciously in every waking moment.

Let's review a few practical approaches to "right surrender." In order to move toward the mindful acceptance of all things you encounter, try the following exercise. Take regular walks through both attractive and unattractive surroundings. The attractive surroundings might be whatever you are drawn to—a forest, a park, and so on. Likewise, purposely walk through places you find repulsive—perhaps a garbage-strewn dump site or an ugly strip mall. Make a conscious choice to accept everything you experience or see: the lovely flowers as well as the broken-down rusty car that you pass; the person who smiles at you and also the one walking down the street cursing and looking at you strangely. Accept all of these things as perfect manifestations of Nuit. Repeat as needed. It sounds simple, and it is, but it's not especially *easy*—so challenge yourself to do this on a day-to-day basis and see what you get.

Similarly, note in your diary when you experience a strong attraction to or repulsion from particular people, outer events, or inner experiences. Don't reflexively accept pleasant experiences as "good" or unpleasant ones as "bad." Rather, strive to accept each experience on an equal footing, using this "radical acceptance" as one more tool in your arsenal of devotional practices aimed at Nuit. Any reflexive moving toward or pushing away based on mere *feeling* is by definition a limiting action of the *ruach* or *nephesh*; and if you can interrupt that process just long enough to acknowledge that whatever is happening to you *right now* is a necessary aspect of your experience, and actively choose to embrace it as such, you can open a door into a more meaningful and transcendent experience of your world.

Another technique is to make a list of your own perceived strengths and weaknesses. Then, one by one, review each of them and try to see how each serves your True Will—especially your weaknesses! This service to

True Will may take the form of some inner asset you have overlooked, or it may simply be that committing yourself to growth in a particular area of weakness eventually opens up that area as a new strength. Such a practice allows you to eventually move toward full acceptance of all that you are. Just as we must strive to be fully accepting of outer experience, we must be fully accepting of all the parts of our inner being—all the triumphs and pitfalls of our psyche. If we fail to do this, we are effectively walling off parts of ourselves and relegating them to the shadow. This tends to result in unconscious projections of such shadow material, and a denial of who and what we really are—a manifestation of Nuit, coequal with, and as beautiful as, any star in the heavens. In your path toward K&C of the HGA you will undoubtedly find that *all you are* is utilized and put into service of the True Will, so the sooner you can take conscious ownership of the totality of your being, the more you will be on track toward K&C.

I'd like to close this discussion with a poem by my teacher Soror Meral (Phyllis Seckler) called "The Adoration of Nuit":

I adore Thee, Nuit, I adore the agonies and trials,
I adore the deadly deep desperation,
The uneven sleepless nights, vials
Of Thy eternal loneliness in manifestation.

I adore Thee through all that happens.
I am a quintessence of soul set on fire,
A flaming up of inner aspirations,
Forming a true eidolon of a soul that aspires.

I adore Thee Nuit, I adore Thy sweet traces
Of ineffable love, hidden in unlimited space
And hidden in life's sorrowful faces.
I adore Thee through life's race.

O, golden and silver of life's mystic dawn!
We move as a faint spark of light in vast illumination;
Thus sparking and living know how we spawn
Phenomena and all its illusion.

I adore Thee, Nuit, oh vast expanding One
Of illimitable Space. I in Thy bosom a minute
Vestige of forgotten and unknown atom
Spell yet an end to notions of the finite.

Oh, vast blue Space, O signature of matter,
Oh unfulfilled in eternal grace!
Who yearn for dancing point of light, unshattered
By its law of gravity and place.

Still I adore Thee, adore Thee, adore Thee,
Everlasting management of possibilities.
Adore Thy oneness and interpenetration of me,
Adore Thy ineffable harmonies.

Oh, plentiful agency of limitless beauty,
I adore Thee far into blue-dimpled night,
I bend towards Thee in evanescent duty
As a spark to manifest life, love, liberty and light.

I adore Thee as my true soul steals forth;
I adore Thee in art and inspiration;
I adore Thee in all loves and silent mirth;
I adore Thee in quiet transformation.

I am a virgin earth unto Thy sublime expression,
A virgin Queen, Malkah unrecognized.
I adore Thy traces through me in secret recognition
Of Illumination at last by Thee franchised.

Oh, Nuit, Goddess of all and none
And one again, and whatever may be
On heaven and earth and all between.
I love Thee because I am Thy whole-made Tree.

In Thy dispensation I am seeing through
Thy veils of dance as disguised infinity
As mysterious as eagle that flew
Into thine Empyrean, dissolving his trinity.

A soul laid bare aspires yet again to Thy bosom
Amid all of illusions laid aside and abandoned
Until the least of these lead to love's fruition
Beyond all experience that may be fathomed.

Oh, Nuit, I in Thy embrace lie serene
And turned into Nothing, only a cenotaph
Marking my existence. Too glorious to bear
Is Nuit who annihilates thus even my path.

This path exists no more because swallowed
In essential space. I am the butterfly
Destroyed by Light, wings that were malleable
To circumstance are gone in ecstasy of death's blight.

I adore Thee, Nuit, Thou glorious One unfulfilled
Through every interstice of space.
Today and always this life is spilled
In ecstasy of Thine unwearying embrace.[31]

---

[31] Seckler, P. (2017). *Collected Poems 1946–1996*. D. Shoemaker & L. Gardner (Eds.). Sacramento: Temple of the Silver Star, 92–5.

PART TWO

*Thelemic Practice
in Detail*

CHAPTER 8

ADVANCED THELEMIC MEDITATIONS

The basics of meditation in the A∴A∴ system are practiced as early as the Probationer grade. The work gradually builds across the Neophyte and Zelator grades, and it is expected that the aspirant of these early grades will maintain a consistent daily practice of raja yoga including *asana* (posture), *dharaṇa* (concentration), and (especially at Zelator) *pranayama* (breath control). While *pranayama* and *asana* are tested at Zelator, there is no formal testing in *dharaṇa* or other more advanced meditation until the Practicus grade and beyond. Because of this, many aspirants exploring Crowley's instructional practices tend to have much less exposure to, and practical experience with, these advanced meditation practices as compared to the foundational instructions in *Liber E* and other introductory libers. This chapter will focus on several of these lesser-known practices, giving tips for performance and insight into potential results.

I strongly recommend that you prepare for what follows by reviewing *Liber E*, as well as the *Living Thelema* chapter on meditation and visualization. I will assume that you have familiarity with the various terms from raja yoga in my discussion here. I will also assume that you are well versed in the terminology of the sephiroth and paths of the Tree of Life, and the grades of A∴A∴. Finally, I will assume that you are competent in basic relaxation, posture, and concentration practices as you approach the work of this chapter. It's important to keep in mind that these particular practices are some of the most subtle in the system, with results that are quite subjective and highly individualized. Accordingly, please take my comments as suggestive of the general type of results you might expect, not concrete descriptions of "success"; and of course, as always, if you are working under supervision in a structured system, your designated teachers should be your primary guides.

Liber BATRACHOPHRENOBOOCOSMOMACHIA

Liber BATRACHOPHRENOBOOCOSMOMACHIA, "The Battle of the Frog, the Mind, the Roar, and the Universe,"[32] is assigned to the Practicus of A∴A∴ as an exercise in the expansion of the mind. This is a fitting goal for the Practicus, whose work relates in many ways to the path of gnana yoga, "union through knowledge." The primary practical technique in the liber involves increasingly intense and expansive visualizations of the solar system and beyond, and is thus numbered 536, the value of the Hebrew word *masloth*, referring to the "sphere of fixed stars." It may not immediately be apparent why such visualizations might assist in the aspirant's path toward K&C, but if we stop to consider how expansion of our sense of the *scope and scale* of our mind exalts our sense of the true trans-egoic spiritual Self, the utility becomes more clear. Every step we take toward disidentifying with ego-consciousness is a step toward *cosmic* consciousness; and stretching the mind to its limits through labor-intensive visualization practices such as these aids in instilling in us the awe such consciousness should inspire.

---

[32] In Crowley, A. (1993). *The Equinox*, Vol. I, No. 10. York Beach, ME: Weiser, 35–40.

Let's review some key passages from this liber.

0. Let the Practicus study the textbooks of astronomy, travel, if need be, to a land where the sun and stars are visible, and observe the heavens with the best telescopes to which he may have access. Let him commit to memory the principal facts, and (at least roughly) the figures of the science.

1. Now, since these figures will leave no direct impression with any precision upon his mind, let him adopt this practice A.

A. Let the Practicus be seated before a bare square table, and let an unknown number of small similar objects be thrown by his chela[33] from time to time upon the table, and by that chela be hastily gathered up.
Let the Practicus declare at the glance, and the chela confirm by his count, the number of such objects.

The practice should be for a quarter of an hour thrice daily. The maximum number of objects should at first be seven. This maximum should increase by one at each practice, provided that not a single mistake is made by the Practicus in appreciating the number thrown.

This practice should continue assiduously for at least one year.

The quickness of the chela in gathering up the objects is expected to increase with time. The practice need not be limited to a quarter of an hour thrice daily after a time, but increased with discretion. Care must be taken to detect the first symptoms of fatigue, and to stop, if possible, even before it threatens. The practised psychologist learns to recognise even minute hesitations that mark the forcing of the attention.

---

[33] An assistant.

This particular "practised psychologist" detects another example of Crowleyan hyperbole in the recommendations here, in terms of the availability and patience of the *chela*, and the necessary free time to commit more than a year to this single practice! Nevertheless, it is possible to simplify the practice and still gain much from it. For example, the Practicus can have a small camera ready, throw down a handful of blindly selected objects such as jacks or toy blocks, and quickly take a photo to verify their own guess about the number of objects before gathering them up.

Also, it may not be apparent how the practice above relates to expansion of consciousness. The key is that the magician is forced to "externalize" their awareness in such a reactive, immediate, and intense burst, with such repetition, that there is a type of "merging" of consciousness with the objects themselves. Over time, this expands their actual sense of selfhood, and the available reach of their mind.

> 2. *Alternating with the above, let the Practicus begin this practice B. It is assumed that he has thoroughly conquered the elementary difficulties of Dharana, and is able to prevent mental pictures from altering shape, size and colour against his will.*[34]

> *B. Seated in the open air, let him endeavour to form a complete mental picture of himself and his immediate surroundings. It is important that he should be in the centre of such picture, and able to look freely in all directions. The finished picture should be a complete consciousness of the whole fixed, clear, and definite.*

> *Let him gradually add to this picture by including objects more and more distant, until he have an image of the whole field of vision.*

---

[34] See Crowley's *Liber E*, and the chapter of *Living Thelema* on meditation and visualization practices.

He will probably discover that it is very difficult to increase the apparent size of the picture as he proceeds, and it should be his most earnest endeavour to do so. He should seek in particular to appreciate distances, almost to the point of combatting the laws of perspective.

One of the difficulties of this practice is similar to that found in astral or etheric projection, in that it is sometimes unpredictably challenging to "see" or "turn" in particular directions. This is a trainable skill, but it often requires a certain breakthrough of technique unique to each magician, and much practice, to master it.

3. These practices A and B accomplished, and his studies in astronomy completed, let him attempt this practice C.

C. Let the Practicus form a mental picture of the Earth, in particular striving to realize the size of the Earth in comparison with himself, and let him not be content until by assiduity he has well succeeded.

Let him add the moon, keeping well in mind the relative sizes of, and the distance between, the planet and its satellite.

He will probably find the final trick of the mind to be a constant disappearance of the image, and the appearance of the same upon a smaller scale. This trick he must outwit by constancy of endeavour.

He will then in add in turn Venus, Mars, Mercury and the Sun.

It is permissible at this stage to change the point of view to the centre of the Sun, and to do so may add stability to the conception.

The Practicus may then add the Asteroids, Jupiter, Saturn, Uranus and Neptune. The utmost attention to detail is now

necessary, as the picture is highly complex, apart from the
difficulty of appreciating relative size and distance.

Let this picture be practised month after month until it
is absolutely perfect.[35] *The tendency which may manifest*
itself to pass into Dhyana and Samadhi must be resolutely
combated with the whole strength of the mind.

Let the Practicus then re-commence the picture, starting
from the Sun, and adding the planets one by one, each with
its proper motion, until he have an image perfect in all
respects of the Solar System as it actually exists. Let him
particularly note that unless the apparent size approximate
to the real, his practice is wasted. Let him then add a comet
to the picture; he may find, perhaps that the path of this
comet may assist him to expand the sphere of his mental
vision until it include a star.

And thus, gathering one star after another, let his contem-
plation become vast as the heaven, in space and time ever
aspiring to the perception of the Body of Nuit; yea, the
Body of Nuit.

One very useful tool for this progressive visualization process is
NASA/JPL's Solar System Simulator, which can display views of the sun,
moon, and planets to and from each other, with quite a few other vari-
able settings. This, combined with easily obtainable images of the relative
sizes and distances between the bodies, should enable you to more easily
create the necessary inner experience. You might find it helpful to create
a series of images, moving from planet to planet, and then spend a good
bit of time meditating on each of these before each session of practice
C. While these outer visual representations are no replacement for the

---

[35] This is, in my estimation, a bit of classic Crowleyan hyperbole.

practice itself, they can be a rough template for the inner work. With extended practice, you will likely be able to "zoom" in or out around all the planets and the Sun, much like on a computer screen, in any direction, while keeping their relative distances from each other and their relative sizes intact.

In reviewing my own experiences with this liber, and those of the students I have supervised over the years, I have drawn a few conclusions about its real import. Firstly, any true expansion of consciousness *requires* an acceptance of our responsibility to the universe, of which we are a part. This responsibility, in turn, implies and requires the love which can only be fully felt when the **unity** of the individual and the universe is recognized. We are all one, from this "Nuit" perspective, and as soon as we *experience* this to be true, we must live our lives in accordance with this experience, or be the worst kind of hypocrite. Secondly, I would emphasize the psychological impact this practice can bring in terms of the simple, but awe-inspiring, realities of physical existence—to really feel oneself strapped to this planet, whirling through the cosmos, and simultaneously be aware of all the other life here: the jungles, the oceans, someone taking a bath in China, another in a high rise in Manhattan; a cold mountain on Mars, a burning sun, and a distant nebula. . . . All one mind, and that mind is each of us, and *all of us*. Every movement of our limbs, every breath in our lungs, is the whirling of a galaxy, and a heartbeat in the body of Nuit.

Liber Turris vel Domus Dei

Liber Turris vel Domus Dei[36] is also known as *The Book of The Tower* or *The Book of The House of God*. "The Book of the Tower" and "The House of God" are two alternate titles that have appeared over the years for Atu 16 in the Thoth deck, The Tower. *Liber Turris* is a Class B document numbered 16, and this of course corresponds to the number of the

---

[36] In Crowley, A. (1993). *The Equinox*, Vol. I, No. 6. York Beach, ME: Weiser, 11–15.

Atu. In the A∴A∴ curriculum, *Liber Turris* is assigned to the Practicus and Philosophus grades. This certainly makes sense, in that the path of Peh connects Hod and Netzach—the two sephiroth associated with the grades of Practicus and Philosophus, respectively.

The symbolism of The Tower Atu itself involves the breaking down of the thought-forms of Hod with the fiery, passionate energy of Netzach, and the interplay between these two poles— the dynamic relationship between intellect and emotion, the rational and the irrational. The card shows a flaming mouth spewing out flame, destroying the tower, and the geometric figures falling out of it symbolize those thought-forms which also need to be destroyed in order to be reformed into new ones. This symbolism parallels the work of the practice itself, for this is an exercise in the destruction of thought. It's really quite an ingenious practice—simple in concept, but certainly a more advanced meditation practice. You've probably experienced in your prior work with meditation that it is far easier to train the mind to focus on *something*, such as an image, the breath, or a mantra, than it is to get the mind to just stop thinking altogether.

How does this practice assist the aspirant on the journey toward K&C of the HGA? What's the practical utility of training the mind in this fashion? By this stage of their work the Practicus has spent years engaged in basic concentration practices, but this is not enough. They must increasingly be able not only to focus thought but to silence it completely. All of the mind-stilling practices of A∴A∴ aim to quiet the chatter of everyday thought; then, in that silence, the aspirant may be able to hear the voice of the HGA with increasing power and clarity.

Let's review the actual instructions of the liber. I will add commentary based on my own experience, and whenever needed to flesh out the intent of various aspects of the practice.

> *0. This practice is very difficult. The student cannot hope for much success unless he has thoroughly mastered Asana and*

obtained much definite success in the meditation practices of
Liber E and Liber HHH.

As a reminder, *Liber E* is the basic instructional practice in yoga, and *Liber HHH* is a three-part guided meditation practice. The first two parts relate to the initiations of the Neophyte and Zelator grades, respectively, and the third part is an instruction in active visualization and energetic work with *kundalini.*

On the other hand, any success in this practice is of an exceed-
ingly high character, and the student is less liable to illusion
and self-deception in this than in almost any other that We
make known.

It is all too easy for beginning students to get some preliminary results in meditation, including having profound ideas or visions flash in their heads. These are actually *breaks* in meditation when approaching it as a mind-stilling practice! In any case, beginners can easily delude themselves about the importance of their results when these are more dramatic or visually impressive; but it's hard to be self-deluded about your results if the only goal is to get your mind to shut up. It's pretty clear if you are succeeding or not, and if you are, it's not going to be heralded by fantastical visions that make you very impressed with yourself. Rather, it will likely manifest as a certain inner stillness, and a discipline of mental training which brings its own broad benefits.

1. First Point. The student should discover for himself the
apparent position of the point in his brain where thoughts
arise, if there be such a point.

If not, he should seek the position of the point where thoughts
are judged.

There's obviously a lot of room for subjective experience here, but it is very possible to identify this thought-origination point, and many find it is toward the lower-middle back of the brain, near the brain stem. I'm not arguing that this is neuroanatomical fact, just subjective experience, as I said. Many perceive that a spot somewhat toward the front from this point is where thoughts are judged or analyzed. As you start to trace this path backward, toward the source of thought, you may discover that it's like going on a sort of a psycho-archaeological dig through your own neural pathways, getting more and more "primal" as you go. There is an impulse toward thought, leading to an analysis of thought, leading to combination with other thoughts, creating increasingly complex thought-forms.

> 2. *Second Point. He must also develop in himself a Will of*
> *Destruction, even a Will of Annihilation. It may be that this*
> *shall be discovered at an immeasurable distance from his phys-*
> *ical body. Nevertheless, this he must reach, with this must he*
> *identify himself even to the loss of himself.*

What often ends up happening is the identification with a destructive force that seems to be "floating" out in front of the head, generating something akin to a lightning bolt that instantaneously wipes out whatever thought was rising. It really is uncannily helpful to have this destructive force externalized—not visualized as an entity or anthropomorphized in any way, just a source of destruction floating out there and zapping every thought as it arises. This seems to aid in the disidentification with the ego and its thoughts, which is a central goal of the Great Work as a whole.

> 3. *Third Point. Let this Will[37] then watch vigilantly the point*
> *where thoughts arise, or the point where they are judged, and*
> *let every thought be annihilated as it is perceived or judged.*
> *[This is also the "Opening of the Eye of Shiva." Ed.]*
>
> 4. *Fourth Point. Next, let every thought be inhibited in its*
> *inception.*

---

[37] That is, the Will to Destruction.

5. Fifth Point. Next, let even the causes or tendencies that if
unchecked ultimate in thoughts be discovered and annihilated.

This is where it gets even trickier—what are these "causes or tendencies"? This calls to mind the meditation practice known as *mahasatti-
patthana*, which is a Buddhist-style observation of breath where one
progressively notes simple sensations, then perception of sensation, then
a consciousness that is doing the perceiving, and so on, essentially "back-
ing up the camera" from your everyday awareness to observe cause after
cause after cause. The effect is somewhat similar to that which is achieved
through practice of *Liber Turris*.

6. Sixth and Last Point. Let the true cause of all [Mayan, the
Magician, or Mara. Also The Dweller on the Threshold in a
very exalted sense. Ed.] be unmasked and annihilated.

7. This is that which was spoken by wise men of old time con-
cerning the destruction of the world by fire; yea, the destruc-
tion of the world by fire.

This is harder to talk about, if it's possible to talk about it at all. We must
seek to discover those seed principles and impulses that lead to the existence
of our own minds! This practice takes the whole concept of meditation to
its ultimate end result—identifying the cause of one's own mental existence,
and the flow of primal thought emerging from universal consciousness itself,
resulting in a little pinpoint of awareness we call an individual mind.

The liber concludes with what is essentially a poetic pep talk to help
the aspirant get into the spirit of the practice:

8. [This and the following verses are modern origin.] Let
the Student remember that each Point represents a definite
achievement of great difficulty.

9. Let him not then attempt the second until he be well satis-
fied of his mastery over the first.

10. This practice is also that which was spoken by Fra. P. in a
parable as follows:

11. Foul is the robber stronghold, filled with hate;
Thief strangling thief, and mate at war with mate,
Fronting wild raiders, all forlorn to Fate!

There is nor health nor happiness therein.
Manhood is cowardice, and virtue sin.
Intolerable blackness hems it in.

Not hell's heart hath so noxious a shade;
Yet harmless and unharmed, and undismayed,
Pines in her prison an unsullied maid.

Penned by the master mage to his desire,
She baffles his seductions and his ire,
Praying God's all-annihilating fire.

The Lord of Hosts gave ear unto her song:
The Lord of Hosts waxed wrathful at her wrong.
He loosed the hound of heaven from its thong.

Violent and vivid smote the levin flash.
Once the tower rocked and cracked beneath its lash,
Caught inextinguishable fire; was ash.

But that same fire that quelled the robber strife,
And struck each being out of lust and life,
Left the mild maiden a rejoicing wife.

12. And this:

13. There is a well before the Great White Throne

That is choked up with rubbish from the ages;
Rubble and clay and sediment and stone,
Delight of lizards and despair of sages.

Only the lightning from His hand that sits,
And shall sit when the usurping tyrant falls,
Can purge that wilderness of wills and wits,
Let spring that fountain in eternal halls.

14. And this:

15. Sulphur, Salt, and Mercury:

Which is master of the three?

Salt is Lady of the Sea;
Lord of Air is Mercury.

Now by God's grace here is salt
Fixed beneath the violet vault.

Now by God's love purge it through
With our right Hermetic dew.

Now by God wherein we trust
Be our sophic salt combust.

Then at last the Eye shall see
Three in One and One in Three,

Sulphur, Salt, and Mercury,
Crowned by Heavenly Alchemy!

To the One who sent the Seven
Glory in the Highest Heaven!

To the Seven who are the Ten
Glory on the Earth, Amen!

16. And of the difficulties of this practice and of the Results that
reward it, let these things be discovered by the right Ingenium
of the Practicus.

Liber Iod

Crowley's *Liber Iod* originally appeared under the title *Liber Tav*[38] (*Liber Vesta* was an even older title), but a brief initial note clarifies its basic attributions: "It is referred to the path of Virgo and the letter Yod." The liber appears on the Dominus Liminis syllabus, and certainly connects to the work of that grade, in that the entirety of the aspirant's work is drawn to a point of focus on the Light of the HGA, in one form or another. The practices it contains serve the Dominus Liminis's task of mastering *prayahara* and *dharana*, the climax of all their work with these disciplines across the prior grades.

Clues about the import and nature of the liber can be gleaned from its numerical coding, 831. In Greek, we find that 831 is the value of words such as *pyramid*, *phallus*, *death*, and even the phrase *Fiat Yod* if rendered in Greek rather than Latin or Hebrew. These all suggest the singular importance of Yod as an emblem of creative power, and the practices of the book all function to concentrate power in similarly singular ways. Furthermore, since Yod is attributed to the lamp-bearing Hermit of the Tarot, we can see a symbolic association with the Magick Lamp, which

---

[38] In Crowley, A. (1993). *The Equinox*, Vol. I, No. 7. York Beach, ME: Weiser, 93–100.

is the magical implement created by the Dominus Liminis. Let's review some specific passages.

> *1. This is the book of drawing all to a point.*

> *2. Herein are described three methods whereby the consciousness of the Many may be melted to that of the One.*

This is not only a reference to the cultivation of a "oneness" of the mind's many streams of thought, but also to the act of uniting the mind of the aspirant to the One Mind of the All-Spirit, the personal representation of which is the aspirant's own HGA.

> *II. FIRST METHOD*

> *0. Let a magical circle be constructed, and within it an upright Tau drawn upon the ground. Let this Tau be divided into 10 squares (see Liber CMLXIII, Illustration 1).*

> *1. Let the magician be armed with the Sword of Art. [This ritual is preferably performed by the Adept as an Hermit armed with wand and lamp, instead of as in text. –N.]*

> *2. Let him wear the black robe of a Neophyte.*

> *3. Let a single flame of camphor burn at the top of the Tau, and let there be no other light or ornament. [This ritual is preferably performed by the Adept as an Hermit armed with wand and lamp, instead of as in text. –N.]*

> *4. Let him "open" the Temple as in DCLXXI, or in any other convenient manner.*

This last comment refers to the various versions of the "Opening by Pyramid" shown in *Liber Pyramidos* and *Liber Throa* (both numbered 671), but as Crowley says, any effective temple opening may be chosen.

5. Standing at the appropriate quarters, at the edge of the
circle, let him banish the 5 elements by the appropriate rituals.

I recommend the Greater Banishing Rituals of the Pentagram corresponding to the elements of Spirit, Fire, Water, Air, and Earth. (See
Living Thelema, Liber O,[39] and elsewhere.)

6. Standing at the edge of the circle, let him banish the 7 plan-
ets by the appropriate rituals. Let him face the actual position
of each planet in the heavens at the time of his working.

I recommend the Greater (sometimes called Supreme) Banishing
Rituals of the Hexagram, corresponding to the seven classical planets.
(Again, see *Living Thelema, Liber O*, and elsewhere.)

7. Let him further banish the twelve signs of the Zodiac by the
appropriate rituals, facing each sign in turn.

Use the zodiacal forms of the Greater Banishing Rituals of the Hexagram (i.e., using the hexagrams of the ruling planet, but with the glyph
and corresponding colors of the desired zodiacal sign rather than the
planet).

8. Let him at each of these 24 banishings make three cir-
cumambulations widdershins, with the signs of Horus and
Harpocrates in the East as he passes it.

These widdershins circumambulations serve as additional *physical* acts
of banishing, emphasizing each of the *ritual* banishings.

9. Let him advance to the square of Malkuth in the Tau, and
perform a ritual of banishing Malkuth. But here let him not

---

[39] In Crowley, A. (1997). *Magick: Liber ABA* (2nd rev. ed.). Hymenaeus Beta (Ed.). York
Beach, ME: Red Wheel/Weiser, LLC.

leave the square to circumambulate the circle, but use the for-
mula and God-form of Harpocrates.

10. Let him advance in turn to the squares Jesod, Hod, Net-
zach, Tiphereth, Geburah, Chesed, and banish each by appro-
priate rituals.

11. And let him know that such rituals include the pronunci-
ation of the appropriate names of God backwards, and also a
curse against the Sephira in respect of all that which it is, for
that which distinguishes and separates it from Kether.

These sephirothic banishings may usefully employ the Greater Banishing Rituals of the Hexagram, with the Hebrew hierarchies corresponding to the sephiroth rather than the planets; that is, the names of gods,
archangels, angelic choirs, and the relevant "Heavens of Assiah." Crowley's suggestion to pronounce names backwards and curse the non-Kether
sephiroth certainly puts a twist on the usual procedures! The obvious
implication is that the magician is treating Kether as the One/No Thing
into which all other things (including the magician themselves) are being
withdrawn.

12. Advancing to the squares of Binah and Chokmah in turn,
let him banish these also. And for that by now an awe and
trembling shall have taken hold upon him, let him banish
these by a supreme ritual of inestimable puissance. And let him
beware exceedingly lest his will falter or his courage fail.

I suggest utilizing the hexagram of Saturn for banishing these supernal sephiroth, and amending the procedure with the same "backwards-
cursing" technique described in the last point.

13. Finally, let him, advancing to the square of Kether, banish
that also by what means he may. At the end whereof let him set
his foot upon the light, extinguishing it [If armed with wand

*and lamp let him extinguish the light with his hand. –N.];
and, as he falleth, let him fall within the circle.*

III. SECOND METHOD

*1. Let the Hermit be seated in his Asana, robed, and let him
meditate in turn upon every several part of his body until that
part is so unreal to him that he no longer includes it in his com-
prehension of himself. For example if it be his right foot, let him
touch that foot, and be alarmed, thinking, "A foot! . . . foot!
What is this foot? Surely I am not alone in the Hermitage!"
And this practice should be carried out not only at the time of
meditation, but during the day's work.*

*2. This meditation is to be assisted by reasoning; as "This
foot is not I. If I should lose my foot, I should still be I. This
foot is a mass of changing and decaying flesh, bone, skin,
blood, lymph, etc. while I am the Unchanging and Immortal
Spirit, uniform, not made, unbegotten, formless, self-
luminous," etc.*

*3. This practice being perfect for each part of the body, let him
combine his workings until the whole body is thus understood
as the non-Ego and as illusion.*

*4. Let then the Hermit, seated in his Asana, meditate upon the
Muladhara cakkra and its correspondence as a power of the
mind, and destroy it in the same manner as aforesaid. Also by
reasoning: "This emotion (memory, imagination, intellect, will,
as it may be) is not I. This emotion is transient: I am immov-
able. This emotion is passion. I am peace." And so on.*

*Let the other Cakkrams in their turn be thus destroyed, each
one with its mental or moral attribute.*

The chapter on chakras in *Living Thelema* may be suggestive for understanding these "mental or moral" attributes.

> 5. In this let him be aided by his own psychological analysis, so that no part of his conscious being be thus left undestroyed. And on his thoroughness in this matter may turn his success.

Strive to define with precision the full meaning of each of these "zones" of self, so that you know just as precisely what you are attempting to banish! The closing exercise from the first chapter of the present volume might also be used to good effect here.

> 6. Lastly, having drawn all his being into the highest Sahasrara Cakkra, let him remain eternally fixed in meditation thereupon.

> 7. Aum.

IV. THIRD METHOD

> 1. Let the Hermit stimulate each of the senses in turn, concentrating upon each until it ceases to stimulate. [The senses of sight and touch are extremely difficult to conquer. In the end the Hermit must be utterly unable by any effort to see or feel the object of those senses. O.M.]

There's that Crowleyan instructional hyperbole again; but give it a shot!

> 2. This being perfected, let him combine them two at a time. For example, let him chew ginger (taste and touch), and watch a waterfall (sight and hearing), and watch incense (sight and smell), and crush sugar in his teeth (taste and hearing), and so on.

3. These twenty-five practices being accomplished, let him combine them three at a time, then four at a time.

4. Lastly, let him combine all the senses in a single object. And herein may a sixth sense be included. He is then to withdraw himself entirely from all the stimulations, perinde ac cadaver, in spite of his own efforts to attach himself to them.

5. By this method it is said that the demons of the Ruach, that is, thoughts and memories, are inhibited, and We deny it not. But if so be that they arise, let him build a wall between himself and them according to the method.

6. Thus having stilled the voices of the Six, may he sense the subtlety of the Seventh.

7. Aum.

[We add the following, contributed by a friend at that time without the A∴A∴ and its dependent orders. He worked out the method himself, and we think it may prove useful to many. O.M.]

(1) The beginner must first practise breathing regularly through the nose, at the same time trying hard to imagine that the breath goes to the Ajna and not to the lungs.

The Prana yama exercises described in the Equinox Vol. I, No. 4, p. 101, must next be practised, always with the idea that Ajna is breathing.

Try to realise that power, not air, is being drawn into the Ajna, is being concentrated there during Kumbhaka, and is vivifying the Ajna during expiration. Try rather to increase the force of concentration in Ajna than to increase so excessively the length of Kumbhaka, as this is dangerous if rashly undertaken.

(2) Walk slowly in a quiet place; realise that the legs are moving, and study their movements. Understand thoroughly that these movements are due to nerve messages sent down from the brain, and that the controlling power lies in the Ajna. The legs are automatic, like those of a wooden monkey: the power in Ajna is that which does the work, is that which walks. This is not hard to realise, and should be grasped firmly, ignoring all other walking sensations.

Apply this method to every other muscular movement.

(3) Lie flat on the back with the feet under a heavy piece of furniture. Keeping the spine straight and the arms in a line with the body, rise slowly to a sitting posture, by means of the force residing in the Ajna (i.e. try to prevent the mind dwelling on any other exertion or sensation).

Then let the body slowly down to its original position. Repeat this two or three times every night and morning, and slowly increase the number of repetitions.

This practice was so effective for me that I began to perceive something like a "warm tickle" at Ajna while performing it. The greater the physical exertion, the more powerful was the perception.

(4) Try to transfer all bodily sensations to the Ajna: e.g. "I am cold" should mean "I feel cold," or better still, "I am aware of a sensation of cold"—transfer this to the Ajna, "The Ajna is aware," etc.

(5) Pain if very slight may easily be transferred to the Ajna after a little practice. The best method for a beginner is to

*imagine he has a pain in the body and then imagine that it
passes directly into the Ajna. It does not pass through the intervening structures, but goes direct. After continual practice even
severe pain may be transferred to the Ajna.*

*(6) Fix the mind on the base of the spine and then gradually
move the thoughts upwards to the Ajna. (In this meditation
Ajna is a Holy of Holies, but it is dark and empty.)*

*Finally, strive hard to drive anger and other obsessing thoughts
into the Ajna. Try to develop a tendency to think hard of Ajna
when these thoughts attack the mind, and let Ajna conquer them.*

*Beware of thinking of "My Ajna." In these meditations and
practices, Ajna does not belong to you; Ajna is the master and
worker, you are the wooden monkey.*

This last practice—the intense focus on the Ajna chakra as the source
of power, and the real master, of all of the mind and body—while presented almost as an afterthought in this liber, is in my estimation the
most powerful tool in the entire book. My own practice of *Liber Iod*
overlapped with an incredibly challenging period of my life. Soror Meral
had just died, and I was visiting my own dying father for the last time. My
marriage was also ending—another form of death. The modes and shades
of grief involved during this period were myriad; but I decided to wrap it
all right into my work with *Liber Iod*. In addition to the other Ajna-fo-
cused practices described above, I resolved to "drive" the grief into Ajna.
I performed daily *dharana* practices focused on breathing through Ajna,
as a form of purifying this grief. There was a simultaneous awareness of
the Magick Lamp at the Sahasrara chakra, as well. My wedding date with
the HGA was fast approaching—only about three months away, though
I didn't know it yet—and all these practices became a perpetual, eternal
living of the Will and walking of the path of the Angel, in every emotion,
thought, word, and deed.

My work with "body disidentification" went quickly and perfectly well—I had practiced similar exercises for years. The chakra disidentification was slower, more methodical, more difficult, but no less successful. After progressing through the seven, there would be fleeting moments of distraction, but I was able to more or less immediately identify these distractions as one or another of the chakras attempting to reassert itself: for example, a stirring of sexual images in Svadisthana after thinking of a lover for a moment, or a brief thought of hypothetically being chastised by Soror Meral for an incomplete diary practice (i.e., Manipura asserting itself, perceiving a threat to my integrity and emotional safety from without), and so on.

In my case, at least, the central tasks of the Dominus Liminis—abiding on the threshold, control of intuition and aspiration, control of thought—all these were elicited by the life tests placed before me. I was severely and repeatedly challenged to keep my focus on my HGA and only my HGA. The exact *method* of keeping my focus there, however, was not to be found *anywhere* other than by using my own intuition, which had to be rightly wielded and controlled in order to find the solution. All of this was a vital and intense lesson in the deeper purpose and nature of *Liber Iod*, the Dominus Liminis grade, and the Great Work of personal transformation itself.

Liber Thisharb

Liber Thisharb[40] is initially assigned to the Zelator, but is primarily an instruction of the Adeptus Exemptus grade. It first appeared in *The Equinox*, Vol. I, No. 7, and then again in *Magick in Theory and Practice*. The non-word title of the liber, *Thisharb*, is the Hebrew *berashith*, "in the beginning," spelled in reverse, and is a somewhat cheeky reference to the first word of Genesis. This is in keeping with both the liber's content and its process, since it constitutes an instruction in following the "river of

---

[40] In Crowley, A. (1993). *The Equinox*, Vol. I, No. 7. York Beach, ME: Weiser, 105–116.

the soul" upstream (i.e., in reverse) to its source, thereby acquiring deeper knowledge about the True Will, so-called "past lives," and more.

The initial appearance of the liber on the Zelator syllabus makes perfect sense, as the Zelator is tasked with deepening their awareness of True Will; but it connects even more deeply with the work of the Adeptus Exemptus, who, abiding in Chesed but facing the Abyss, must strive to find the transpersonal and transrational seed principles that explain their past and present incarnations—the infinite "river" of True Will. Consider the following comments, drawn from my commentary on my visions of the Enochian Aethyrs in *The Winds of Wisdom*:

> *The particular dimensions of a capstone are sufficient to define the shape of the pyramid below. Just so, the seed of Self resident in* neshamah *defines the 'shape' of the personality which developes to serve it. The Adeptus Exemptus, having brought the* ruach *(the pyramid, in this metaphor) to its full potential, must then discover the 'capstone' or Seed which explains and defines all that they have been in mortal life. In some senses, this Seed represents the expansion of the True Will concept into the realm of the infinite—that is, the universal motive behind the particularized expression of Will that has been lived out at the level of the individual incarnation.*

> *The Adeptus Exemptus is a perfected human, in the usual sense. They have attained to the pinnacle of their field; they are well-known due to their excellence, and their published works, whether strictly so or not. Yet they are not able to completely revolutionize the world in which they live, for they have not yet fully and consciously become a vessel of Universal Will. Once they turn themselves over into the Cup of Babalon, and are willing to give up all they have to the service of the One Will, they attain to Binah. Then, and only then, can they lead others by their own light (outwardly); for inwardly they are simply*

shining forth with the light of Universal Will that they have only now become able to wield.

As Adeptus Exemptus they were limited by their vision of self and its relation to the universe. Their light was dimmer, and could only attract (energetically) those within a certain subset of their field—a school of thought, such as a theoretical orientation within psychotherapy or physics. The Magister Templi, on the other hand, will be the voice of a completely new vision, a complete paradigm shift in human consciousness of some type. These are the Isaac Newtons, the Aristotles, and the Picassos of the world. Yet there is more growth to come. The Magister Templi must then discover the seed principle (deeper still than the "capstone seed" sought by the [Adeptus Exemptus]) by which they were impregnated. What was the Word which, when planted in the soil of Binah, grew into the garden tended by the Magister?

The Magus has identified with that original motive principle, and has the Wisdom to see its inevitability—the necessity of its being. Their presence in the world is the seed of growth and change—of evolution itself. That is, their mere presence simply changes things, entirely in accord with the Universal Will which they ARE, consciously and (behaviorally speaking) reliably.[41]

Let's review some key passages from *Liber Thisharb*; I will comment with potentially useful reflections, where appropriate.

0. This book is not intended to lead to the supreme attainment. On the contrary, its results define the separate being of the

---

[41] Shoemaker, D. (2016). *The Winds of Wisdom: Visions from the Thirty Enochian Aethyrs.* Sacramento: Anima Solis Books, 59–61.

> *Exempt Adept from the rest of the Universe, and discover his*
> *relation to that Universe.*
>
> *1. It is of such importance to the Exempt Adept that We cannot*
> *overrate it. Let him in no wise adventure the plunge into the*
> *Abyss until he have accomplished this to his most perfectest*
> *satisfaction.*

As I have noted in other places, concerning the work of the Exempt Adept, until they fully know themselves in their fullness as an incarnate human *ruach*, and understand the "relation" of that individual self to the universal All, no full offering of self is possible. Partial attainment here amounts to offering a few drops of our blood into the Grail of Babalon, rather than every drop we possess, as it must be to truly achieve success.

> *2. For in the Abyss no effort is anywise possible. The Abyss is*
> *passed by virtue of the mass of the Adept and his Karma. Two*
> *forces impel him: (1) the attraction of Binah, (2) the impulse*
> *of his Karma; and the ease and even the safety of his passage*
> *depend on the strength and direction of the latter.*
>
> *3. Should one rashly dare the passage, and take the irrevoca-*
> *ble Oath of the Abyss, he might be lost therein through Æons*
> *of incalculable agony; he might even be thrown back upon*
> *Chesed, with the terrible Karma of failure added to his origi-*
> *nal imperfection.*

This illustrates a point about the Oath of the Abyss that I find is often misunderstood. Crowley does indeed state in places that anyone is free to take the Oath and "claim the grade" of Magister Templi. However, this does *not* mean that simply taking the oath actually *confers* the grade. If that were truly the case, the efficiency-minded Crowley would have designed the system of A∴A∴ to consist of one task alone: "Take the Oath!" Since this is certainly not what he did, we can safely infer that he felt other tasks, tools, and tests are nearly always necessary for true attainment of Binah, as the quotes from this portion of *Liber Thisharb* emphasize. The misunderstanding of this process explains a great many of the sad, even tragic, failures in the world of modern Thelema, as any cursory internet search will reveal; occultists who have prematurely taken the Oath, and gone on to embarrass themselves at the least, and destroy their mental or physical health at worst. How many magicians have you met who openly claim to be Masters of the Temple, and whose life and works truly seem to reflect such mastery?[42]

> *4. It is even said that in certain circumstances it is possible to fall altogether from the Tree of Life, and to attain the Towers of the Black Brothers. But We hold that this is not possible for any adept who has truly attained his grade, or even for any man who has really sought to help humanity even for a single second [Those in possession of Liber CLXXXV (the oath papers) will note that in every grade but one the aspirant is pledged to serve his inferiors in the Order.], and that although his aspiration have been impure through vanity or any similar imperfection.*

It is absolutely true, in my experience, that *most* aspiring magicians approach the work with one or more ego-weaknesses in the driver's seat— lust for personal power, a quest for compensation for underlying low self-esteem, or even simply a desire to learn to cast a well-crafted Fireball spell. It is also true that those who persist in the path end up (consciously or not) serving others through their own growth process. Eventually, they tend to realize that the silly ego-goals that brought them to the doorstep of the Great Work have been replaced by the actual fruits of the journey.

---

[42] A favorite story of Soror Meral's involved her being approached by a young man at a social event full of Thelemites. He whispered conspiratorially into her ear, "You know, I'm a Ma-goose," meaning to say "Magus." She simply chuckled and replied, "You certainly are!" Friends, I beg you: Don't be a Ma-goose!

5. Let the Adept who finds the result of these meditations
unsatisfactory refuse the Oath of the Abyss, and live so that
his Karma gains strength and direction suitable to the task at
some future period.

Aspirants who are impatient, at *any* stage of the work, tend to get
ahead of themselves, miss the essential tools, and actually slow their progress down compared to where they would be if they had taken a more
patient and methodical approach. Learn the alphabet before you try to
write poetry!

6. Memory is essential to the individual consciousness; other-
wise the mind were but a blank sheet on which shadows are
cast. But we see that not only does the mind retain impressions,
but that it is so constituted that its tendency is to retain some
more excellently than others. Thus the great classical scholar,
Sir Richard Jebb, was unable to learn even the schoolboy
mathematics required for the preliminary examination at
Cambridge University, and a special act of the authorities was
required in order to admit him.

7. The first method to be described has been detailed in Bhik-
khu Ananda Metteya's "Training of the Mind" (EQUINOX,
I. 5, pp. 28–59, and especially pp. 48–56).[43] *We have little to*
alter or to add. Its most important result, as regards the Oath
of the Abyss, is the freedom from all desire or clinging to any-
thing which it gives. Its second result is to aid the adept in the
second method, by supplying him with further data for his
investigation.

8. The stimulation of memory useful in both practices is also
achieved by simple meditation (Liber E), in a certain stage

---

[43] I.e., Crowley, A. (1993). *The Equinox*, Vol. I, No. 5. York Beach, ME: Weiser, 28–59.

*of which old memories arise unbidden. The adept may then
practise this, stopping at that stage, and encouraging instead of
suppressing the flashes of memory.*

The cultivation of enhanced, everyday memory is a worthy goal in
and of itself, but as we read on we see that Crowley has his sights set far
beyond this.

*9. Zoroaster has said, "Explore the River of the Soul, whence
or in what order you have come; so that although you have
become a servant to the body, you may again rise to that
Order (the A∴A∴) from which you descended, joining Works
(Kamma) to the Sacred Reason (the Tao)."*

*10. The Result of the Second Method is to show the Adept to
what end his powers are destined. When he has passed the
Abyss and become NEMO, the return of the current causes
him "to appear in the Heaven of Jupiter as a morning star or
as an evening star." [The formula of the Great Work "Solve
et Coagula" may be thus interpreted. Solve, the dissolution
of the Self in the Infinite; Coagula, the presentation of the
Infinite in a concrete form to the outer. Both are necessary
to the Task of a Master of the Temple.] In other words, he
should discover what may be the nature of his work. Thus
Mohammed was a Brother reflected into Netzach, Buddha a
Brother reflected into Hod, or, as some say, Daath. The present manifestation of Frater P. to the outer is in Tiphereth, to
the inner in the path of Leo.*

*11. First Method. Let the Exempt Adept first train himself to
think backwards by external means, as set forth here following.*

(a) Let him learn to write backwards, with either hand.

(b) Let him learn to walk backwards.

(c) Let him constantly watch, if convenient, cinematograph films, and listen to phonograph records, reversed, and let him so accustom himself to these that they appear natural, and appreciable as a whole.

(d) Let him practise speaking backwards; thus for "I am He" let him say, "Eh ma I."

(e) Let him learn to read backwards. In this it is difficult to avoid cheating one's self, as an expert reader sees a sentence at a glance. Let his disciple read aloud to him backwards, slowly at first, then more quickly.

(f) Of his own ingenium let him devise other methods.

12. In this his brain will at first be overwhelmed by a sense of utter confusion; secondly, it will endeavour to evade the difficulty by a trick. The brain will pretend to be working backwards when it is really normal. It is difficult to describe the nature of the trick, but it will be quite obvious to anyone who has done practices (a) and (b) for a day or two. They become quite easy, and he will think that he is making progress, an illusion which close analysis will dispel.

13. Having begun to train his brain in this manner, and obtained some little success, let the Exempt Adept, seated in his Asana, think first of his present attitude, next of the act of being seated, next of his entering the room, next of his robing, et cetera, exactly as it happened. And let him most strenuously endeavour to think each act as happening backwards. It is not enough to think: "I am seated here, and before that I was standing, and before that I entered the room," etc. That series is the trick detected in the preliminary practices. The series must not run "ghi-def-abc," but "ihgfedcba": not "horse a is this"

but "esroh a si siht." To obtain this thoroughly well, practice
(c) is useful. The brain will be found to struggle constantly to
right itself, soon accustoming itself to accept "esroh" as merely
another glyph for "horse." This tendency must be constantly
combated.

You will likely find that this "First Method" has a definite "priming" effect on the brain which greatly aids the more advanced practices that follow. At first, the brain is a bit shocked by even superficial practices like writing or walking backwards. There is a peculiar mental stillness that results from this as well, as if the backward movement "cancels out" the usual forward movement, like stirring a pot of soup in one direction, then stopping the current by stirring in the opposite direction. Eventually, with further practice, it will become easier for the perception of time and, indeed, *reality itself,* to flow backward. It should also be noted that in the many years since Crowley wrote these passages, psychophysiological research has repeatedly demonstrated the human brain's remarkable capacity to accommodate to quite severe reversals of perception. One famous example is the experiment in which subjects were given goggles that inverted their vision, making everything appear upside-down. Within a day or two, the subjects' brains had compensated for this, and the world appeared right-side-up again. When the goggles were eventually removed, it took an additional day or two for their brains to revert to normal vision processing. (That must have been quite disconcerting!)

14. In the early stages of this practice the endeavour should be
to meticulous minuteness of detail in remembering actions; for
the brain's habit of thinking forwards will at first be insuper-
able. Thinking of large and complex actions, then, will give a
series which we may symbolically write "opqrstu-hijklmn-ab-
cdefg." If these be split into detail, we shall have "stu-pqr-o—
mn-kl-hij—fg-cde-ab," which is much nearer to the ideal
"utsrqponmlkjihgfedcba."

15. Capacities differ widely, but the Exempt Adept need have no reason to be discouraged if after a month's continuous labour he find that now and again for a few seconds his brain really works backwards.

16. The Exempt Adept should concentrate his efforts upon obtaining a perfect picture of five minutes backwards rather than upon extending the time covered by his meditation. For this preliminary training of the brain is the Pons Asinorum of the whole process.

17. This five minutes' exercise being satisfactory, the Exempt Adept may extend the same at his discretion to cover an hour, a day, a week, and so on. Difficulties vanish before him as he advances; the extension from a day to the course of his whole life will not prove so difficult as the perfecting of the five minutes.

Despite Crowley's warning in #16 about focusing on the last five minutes before extending the time, I found in my own practice that it was useful, even in the very early stages, to play the "movie" of my entire day in reverse, typically when in bed and about to go to sleep. Again, it seemed to serve as a "priming" of the brain for the more challenging work that followed.

18. This practice should be repeated at least four times daily, and progress is shown firstly by the ever easier running of the brain, secondly by the added memories which arise.

19. It is useful to reflect during this practice, which in time becomes almost mechanical, upon the way in which effects spring from causes. This aids the mind to link its memories, and prepares the adept for the preliminary practice of the Second Method.

20. Having allowed the mind to return for some hundred times to the hour of birth, it should be encouraged to endeavour to penetrate beyond that period. If it be properly trained to run backwards, there will be little difficulty in doing this, although it is one of the distinct steps in the practice.

Pushing back past the moment of birth, while not necessarily difficult (with practice), does tend to be preceded by a rising intensity and strain of a sort, until one suddenly seems to "pop" through into a former life— not uncommonly a moment near the death of the previous incarnation.

21. It may be then that the memory will persuade the adept of some previous existence. Where this is possible, let it be checked by an appeal to facts, as follows.

22. It often occurs to men that on visiting a place to which they have never been, it appears familiar. This may arise from a confusion of thought or a slipping of the memory, but it is conceivably a fact.

If, then, the adept "remember" that he was in a previous life in some city, say Cracow, which he has in this life never visited, let him describe from memory the appearance of Cracow, and of its inhabitants, setting down their names. Let him further enter into details of the city and its customs. And having done this with great minuteness, let him confirm the same by consultation with historians and geographers, or by a personal visit, remembering (both to the credit of his memory and its discredit) that historians, geographers, and himself are alike fallible. But let him not trust his memory to assert its conclusions as fact, and act thereupon, without most adequate confirmation.

23. This process of checking his memory should be practised with the earlier memories of childhood and youth by reference

to the memories and records of others, always reflecting upon
the fallibility even of such safeguards.

Crowley's encouragement of skepticism here is, as always, quite
refreshing, especially when it comes to this fraught practice of "past life
regression." After all, there are just a few too many people claiming to
have been Napoleon, Cleopatra, or even Crowley himself to sit comfortably with any reasonably critical thinker. I'm reminded of Karl Germer's
ball-busting comments in a letter to someone making similar claims
(Marcelo Motta) that there are were so many people claiming to be the
reincarnation of Crowley, the avatar of Babalon, or the manifestation of
the "Child of the Prophet" that he wanted to organize Beast, Babalon,
or Child clubs so they could all socialize together . . . far away from him!

24. All this being perfected, so that the memory reaches back
into aeons incalculably distant, let the Exempt Adept med-
itate upon the fruitlessness of all those years, and upon the
fruit thereof, severing that which is transitory and worthless
from that which is eternal. And it may be that he being but an
Exempt Adept may hold all to be savourless and full of sorrow.

25. This being so, without reluctance will he swear the Oath of
the Abyss.

26. Second Method. Let the Exempt Adept, fortified by the
practice of the First Method, enter the preliminary practice of
the Second Method.

27. Second Method. Preliminary Practices. Let him, seated in
his Asana, consider any event, and trace it to its immediate
causes. And let this be done very fully and minutely. Here, for
example, is a body erect and motionless. Let the adept consider
the many forces which maintain it; firstly, the attraction of
the earth, of the sun, of the planets, of the farthest stars, nay,

*of every mote of dust in the room, one of which (could it be
annihilated) would cause that body to move, although so
imperceptibly. Also the resistance of the floor, the pressure of the
air, and all other external conditions. Secondly, the internal
forces which sustain it, the vast and complex machinery of the
skeleton, the muscles, the blood, the lymph, the marrow, all
that makes up a man. Thirdly, the moral and intellectual forces
involved, the mind, the will, the consciousness. Let him continue this with unremitting ardour, searching Nature, leaving
nothing out.*

*28. Next, let him take one of the immediate causes of his posi-
tion, and trace out its equilibrium. For example, the will.
What determines the will to aid in holding the body erect and
motionless?*

*29. This being determined, let him choose one of the forces
which determined his will, and trace out that in similar
fashion; and let this process be continued for many days until
the interdependence of all things is a truth assimilated in his
inmost being.*

*30. This being accomplished, let him trace out his own history
with special reference to the causes of each event. And in this
practice he may neglect to some extent the universal forces
which at all times act on all, as for example the attraction of
masses, and let him concentrate his attention upon the principal and determining or effective causes.*

*For instance, he is seated, perhaps, in a country place in Spain.
Why? Because Spain is warm and suitable for meditation, and
because cities are noisy and crowded. Why is Spain warm? and
why does he wish to meditate? Why choose warm Spain rather
than warm India? To the last question: Because Spain is*

nearer to his home. Then why is his home near Spain? Because
his parents were Germans. And why did they go to Germany?
And so during the whole meditation.

31. On another day, let him begin with a question of another
kind, and every day devise new questions, not only concerning
his present situation, but also abstract questions. Thus let him
connect the prevalence of water upon the surface of the globe with
its necessity to such life as we know, with the specific gravity and
other physical properties of water, and let him perceive ultimately
through all this the necessity and concord of things, not concord as
the schoolmen of old believed, making all things for man's benefit
or convenience, but the essential mechanical concord whose final
law is inertia. And in these meditations let him avoid as if it were
the plague any speculation sentimental or fantastic.

32. Second Method. The Practice Proper. Having then perfected
in his mind these conceptions, let him apply them to his own
career, forging the links of memory into the chain of necessity.

And let this be his final question: To what purpose am I fitted?
Of what service can my being prove to the Brothers of the
A∴A∴ if I cross the Abyss, and am admitted to the City of the
Pyramids?

These are, of course, questions pertaining to the infinite True Will,
and the service to all which it *always* embodies. The thought experiments
presented in the True Will chapter of *Living Thelema* are additional
useful tools in this line of self-questioning.

33. Now that he may clearly understand the nature of this
question, and the method of solution, let him study the reason-
ing of the anatomist who reconstructs an animal from a single
bone. To take a simple example.

34. Suppose, having lived all my life among savages, a ship is cast upon the shore and wrecked. Undamaged among the cargo is a "Victoria." What is its use? The wheels speak of roads, their slimness of smooth roads, the brake of hilly roads. The shafts show that it was meant to be drawn by an animal, their height and length suggest an animal of the size of a horse. That the carriage is open suggests a climate tolerable at any rate for part of the year. The height of the box suggest crowded streets, or the spirited character of the animal employed to draw it. The cushions indicate its use to convey men rather than merchandise; its hood that rain sometimes falls, or that the sun is at times powerful. The springs would imply considerable skill in metals; the varnish much attainment in that craft.

35. Similarly, let the adept consider of his own case. Now that he is on the point of plunging into the Abyss a giant Why? confronts him with uplifted club.

36. There is no minutest atom of his composition which can be withdrawn from him without making him some other than he is; no useless moment in his past. Then what is his future? The "Victoria" is not a waggon; it is not intended for carting hay. It is not a sulky; it is useless in trotting races.

37. So the adept has military genius, or much knowledge of Greek: how do these attainments help his purpose, or the purpose of the Brothers? He was put to death by Calvin, or stoned by Hezekiah; as a snake he was killed by a villager, or as an elephant slain in battle under Hamilcar. How do such memories help him? Until he have thoroughly mastered the reason for every incident in his past, and found a purpose for every item of his present equipment [A Brother known to me was repeatedly baffled in this meditation. But one day

being thrown with his horse over a sheer cliff of forty feet, and
escaping without a scratch or a bruise, he was reminded of his
many narrow escapes from death. These proved to be the last
factors in his problem, which, thus completed, solved itself in
a moment. O.M.], he cannot truly answer even those Three
Questions what were first put to him, even the Three Questions
of the Ritual of the Pyramid; he is not ready to swear the Oath
of the Abyss.

38. But being thus enlightened, let him swear the Oath of the
Abyss; yea, let him swear the Oath of the Abyss.

Since there has been so much discussion of the Oath of the Abyss
in this liber, and in my own comments, I'll conclude this chapter by
reprinting it in its entirety, in the form currently employed in A∴A∴.
I'll note the sephirothic correspondences in brackets, to illustrate
the Oath's structure. The sephirothic nature of the entire Oath is yet
another way in which it serves to identify the Magister Templi as one
who functions in complete harmony with, and as an actual expression
of, the universal will.

I, _____, a member of the Body of God,
hereby bind myself on behalf of the Whole Universe, even as we
are now physically bound unto the cross of suffering:

that I will lead a pure life [Kether], as a devoted servant of the
Order [Chokmah]; that I will understand all things [Binah];

that I will love all things [Chesed]; that I will perform all
things and endure all things [Geburah]; that I will continue in
the Knowledge and Conversation of my Holy Guardian Angel
[Tiphereth];

that I will work without attachment [Netzach]; that I will work in truth [Hod]; that I will rely only upon myself [Yesod];

that I will interpret every phenomenon as a particular dealing of God with my soul. [Malkuth]

And if I fail herein, may my pyramid be profaned, and the Eye closed to me.

CHAPTER 9

CREATING EFFECTIVE
MAGICAL INVOCATIONS

A s is likely apparent to any experienced magician, for a ritual to have any potency whatsoever, the necessary *force* must be invoked with both intensity and specificity. This is the key distinction between a ritual that merely brings chaotic energy into the temple and one which calls forth the one thing needed, with just the right quality and quantity. But before we can look further at how to create such effective invocations, we should clarify the difference between invocation and its close cousin, evocation. Evocation involves calling a spiritual entity into a "Triangle of Art" or similar device, so that we can interact with it *as if* it were entirely external to us. Evocation is generally used for low Yetziratic entities like Goetic spirits, and planetary spirits and intelligences. The magician is in a role of commanding and controlling the spirit. Crowley has an instructive comment concerning evocation in *Magick in Theory and Practice*:

> *The Magician soon discards evocation almost altogether. Only rare circumstances demand any action whatsoever on the material plane. The magician devotes himself entirely to the invocation of a god and as soon as his balance approaches*

perfection, he ceases to invoke any partial god, only that god
vertically above him in his path. A man who perhaps took
up magick merely with the idea of acquiring knowledge, love
or wealth, finds himself irrevocably committed to the perfor-
mance of the great work.[44]

In contrast, invocation is a calling of an entity or force *into* ourselves. Rather than standing in the circle and evoking the spirit into a triangle positioned outside of it, the magician invites the force to fully inhabit themselves, with no separation or externalization. Invocation is generally employed for Atziluthic, Briatic, or high Yetziratic entities such as deities, archangels, angels, and forces of a similar stature. The magician aspires to embody the nature of the force invoked.

In working with both evocation and invocation over the years, I've derived a rule of thumb for deciding between these two approaches for any particular working, and it's served me very well: *If you want all of yourself to be more like the entity*, invoke it. If, on the other hand, *you want the entity to do your bidding and be an extension of yourself*, evoke it. So think about the nature of the entity in question and ask yourself: Do I really want my entire being to take on the character of this force? If your answer to that question is not a resounding yes, then you might want to consider whether it might be more suitable for evocation.

Now that we've clarified the important difference between these two approaches, let's turn our attention to the main focus here, which is of course invocation. There are two primary types of invocation (refer to the chapter in *Living Thelema* on ritual construction for an expanded discussion of these, and how to fit them into a larger ritual structure). *General invocations* bring in undifferentiated magical force, like plugging a TV into a wall socket to get basic power to the device. Examples of this include the Anthem from the Gnostic Mass, or the Preliminary Invocation from

---

[44] In Crowley, A. (1997). *Magick: Liber ABA* (2nd rev. ed.). Hymenaeus Beta (Ed.). York Beach, ME: Red Wheel/Weiser, LLC, 232.

the Goetia used in *Liber Samekh* and elsewhere. Once you have power to the TV, you'll need to tune that TV to the right channel. You need not just generalized force, but the specific *kind* of force pertinent to your ritual aim, and this is a function of the *specific invocation*. There are formal ritual options for this, of course, such as the Greater Rituals of the Pentagram for elemental forces, and of the Hexagram for planetary and zodiacal forces. In addition to, or even instead of, such formal rituals, one might use prayers or poetic invocations devoted to specific gods, such as *Liber Israfel*, which is an invocation of Thoth-Hermes. Regardless of the specific approach you choose, this is your chance to exercise maximum creativity, and utilize every bit of self-knowledge available to you, to tailor your ritual technique exactly as needed.

Let's review a few useful tips regarding specific invocations, so that you can amplify your ability to utilize them with the needed intensity and clarity. I'll annotate my remarks with relevant quotes from *Magick in Theory and Practice*. For the purposes of this discussion, I will assume that you have already done a thorough job of selecting the appropriate force to invoke in the first place, giving careful consideration to the various options of sephiroth and paths. I will also assume that you've constructed a solid ritual framework in which to employ the invocations you've chosen to use. If you need a review on any of these processes, I once again direct you to the chapter on methods of ritual construction in *Living Thelema*.

Let's assume that you've chosen to invoke a deity. It helps to first personify the deity outwardly, and then move toward embodying it. In other words, you begin by relating to the deity as an *external* entity, and then move through a gradual process of increasingly identifying yourself *as* the deity, living out its very nature. First, describe the deity as vividly as possible, using ritualized prose, poetry, or any other such tools. Next, begin to act and speak as the deity would, thereby becoming a veritable talisman of the god. You must make yourself into the proper *form* in order to attract the desired *force*. Refer to *Liber Israfel* for an excellent example of this gradual shifting from outer worship to inner embodiment.

In *Magick in Theory and Practice*, Chapter 15,[45] Crowley gives several useful suggestions for getting "inside the head" of the deity in order to effectively embody it. The first of these is to master the control of your astral body, and then employ that skill to explore symbols and astral realms that correspond to the nature of the deity to be invoked. By doing so, you begin to become more "fluent" in the symbolic language of the deity. He also suggests using a traditional or newly constructed mantra of the deity in your ritual. Rhythmic mantras and chants serve as one way of generating the "energized enthusiasm" required for a ritual to have sufficient force, and a wisely chosen mantra will of course help you connect to the specific force of your chosen deity. Finally, Crowley encourages the magician to employ the astral form of the god at the climax of the ritual, just as you may already be doing in the various adorations of the stations of the sun in *Liber Resh vel Helios*[46] (Ra, Ahathoor, Tum, and Khephra). This assumption of god-forms[47] becomes an indispensable magical technique that you will undoubtedly use over and over in your ritual work. With sufficient practice, you will be able to more or less instantly embody a desired force by assuming its astral shape, like flipping a switch. The same could be said for certain ritual signs and gestures (such as the Sign of the Enterer) which accrue power through a magician's repeated use, enabling them to direct magical force when and where needed. All these tools are in service of my first basic tip: Personify, then embody.

One of the most effective ways to amplify this personification is to take pains to address the multifaceted nature of the deity. In *Liber Astarte*, Crowley suggests a sevenfold structure for such poetic invocations:

> First, an Imprecation, as of a slave unto his Lord.

---

[45] In Crowley, A. (1997). *Magick: Liber ABA* (2nd rev. ed.). Hymenaeus Beta (Ed.). York Beach, ME: Red Wheel/Weiser, LLC.

[46] Ibid., p. 655.

[47] See also Crowley's *Liber O* (Ibid.).

Second, an Oath, as of a vassal to his Liege.

Third, a Memorial, as of a child to his Parent.

Fourth, an Orison, as of a Priest unto his God.

Fifth, a Colloquy, as of a Brother with his Brother.

Sixth, a Conjuration, as to a Friend with his Friend.

Seventh, a Madrigal, as of a Lover to his Mistress.[48]

You can see how these represent seven distinct relational "tones," and if you can explore all of them and flesh them out vibrantly in your invocation, it will tend to amplify its power. How could it be otherwise? Every bit of effort we expend to fully *understand and adore* the force we wish to invoke will help bring it into manifestation with more intensity.

My final primary tip is probably the most important of all: *Enflame yourself in prayer.* Crowley describes this as the whole secret of the process. You must lose yourself in the frenzy of your adoration. Consider Crowley's comments from *Magick in Theory and Practice*:

The mind must be exalted until it loses consciousness of self.
The magician must be carried forward blindly by a force which
although in him and of him is by no means that which he in
his normal state of consciousness calls I. Just as the poet, the
lover or the artist is carried out of himself in a creative frenzy
so must it be for the magician. It is impossible to lay down rules
for the attaining of this special stimulus. To one the mystery
of the whole ceremony may appeal, another may be moved by
the strangeness of the word even by the fact that the barbarous
names are unintelligible to him. Sometimes in the course of
the ceremony the true meaning by some barbarous name that
has hitherto baffled his analysis may flash upon him luminous
and splendid so that he is caught up into orgasm. The smell

---

[48] In Crowley, A. (1997). *Magick: Liber ABA* (2nd rev. ed.). Hymenaeus Beta (Ed.). York Beach, ME: Red Wheel/Weiser, LLC, 628.

of a particular incense may incite him effectively or perhaps the physical ecstasy of the magic dance. Every magician must compose his ceremony in such a manner as to produce a dramatic climax. At the moment when the excitement becomes ungovernable, then the whole conscience being of the magician undergoes a spiritual spasm, at that moment must he utter the supreme maturation. . . . Suppose the supreme invocation to consist of 20 to 30 barbarous names. Let him imagine these names to occupy sections of the vertical column, each double the length of the preceding one. And let him imagine that his consciousness ascends the column with each name. The mere multiplication will then produce a feeling of awe and bewilderment which is the proper forerunner of ecstasy.[49]

Deceptively simple inner tools, but literally mind-blowing when employed correctly. These are truly the inner "calisthenics" necessary to vault yourself into states of spiritual ecstasy, and this is, of course, the essence of enflaming yourself in prayer. Another technique is to stop short of the climax of the ritual repeatedly, by strength of will, again and again and again until it doesn't even occur to you to stop yourself. This too encourages a sufficient level of enflaming. (Did I mention that good ritual technique has a lot in common with good sex?) Crowley comments on this particular phenomenon:

This forgetfulness must be complete, it is fatal to try to let oneself go consciously. . . . Inhibition is no longer possible or even thinkable and the whole being of the magician, no minutest atom saying nay, is irresistibly flung forth, in blinding light amid the roar of ten thousand thunders, the union of God and man is consummated.[50]

---

[49] Ibid., 231–3.

[50] Ibid., 231–2.

Once you have begun the actual invocation, focus *only* on the invocation. Forget about the rest of the ceremony. Failure to do this is one of the most common sources of error in invocation. We fall into the "lust of result," thinking about our ritual aims, whether the ritual is going to work and what we're going to do when we get the desired result. All kinds of messes can occur when we lose sight of simply *bringing in the force*. So we should trust that we have crafted a ritual designed to bring our aim to fruition, and then forget about all that and simply start the ritual "machine" and watch it go. After all, it's fueled by the potency of our invocations!

I want to conclude with some thoughts on a different, but related, plane. If you look at the course of a proper and powerful invocation, it mirrors the process the aspirant goes through in the approach to Adepthood, and the flowering of that Adepthood in their outer life. When you enflame yourself in prayer to your HGA, and you make your whole life into a suitable invocation of the HGA—a talisman of its formula—its force is naturally attracted. You become a veritable "lightning rod" that inevitably draws it forth. The grades of A∴A∴ from Probationer through Dominus Liminis thus serve as an ever-building, long-term enflaming in prayer—not merely through the specific tasks of the different grades, but through the process of crafting *yourself* into the proper form; living your whole life in a "talismanic" state of consciousness, increasingly, so that natural law itself will demand that the presence of your HGA is drawn to your conscious awareness. Then, the wedding with the HGA with K&C is much like the climax of an invocation, when you vault past any conception of the individual self into spiritual ecstasy and, as Crowley states, "the union of god and man is consummated." This of course occurs in the climactic K&C working, but in a much larger sense, that whole surrounding epoch of the life of the Adept will take on the character of this human–divine union. After K&C, the next step for the Adept is to go forth into the world as the prophet of the HGA, attempting to align their every thought, word, and deed with the Angel's message. This is the Adeptus Major grade and beyond, where the entire outer life of the Adept is reshaped as a vessel of True Will. This is the macrocosmic mirror of the process evident in a single ritual; that is, the invocation has come to a climax and you are truly *acting as the deity*.

The skills needed to construct and execute a powerful magical invocation are subtle, and mastery of them is a lifelong endeavor. I hope the basic hints I've given here will be fodder for your own experimentation. Now, go practice!

CHAPTER 10

THE MAGICK OF
THE GNOSTIC MASS

Aleister Crowley's *Liber XV* (The Gnostic Mass)[51] is one of the most beautiful and powerful Thelemic rituals ever created, and since it is performed frequently and publicly around the world it is also, happily, one of the most accessible.[52] It utilizes a specific ritual technology and a definite ritual intention—especially in its context as the central public ritual of Ordo Templi Orientis (O.T.O.) and its ecclesiastical component, Ecclesia Gnostica Catholica, or the Gnostic Catholic Church—but the Mass is also, quite simply, a well-designed magical ritual.

In the first part of this chapter, I'll review the ways in which we can view the Mass as a set of instructions for performing *any* sort of magical

---

[51] In Crowley, A. (1997). *Magick: Liber ABA* (2nd rev. ed.). Hymenaeus Beta (Ed.). York Beach, ME: Red Wheel/Weiser, LLC.

[52] In 2013 e.v., I had the honor and privilege of working with the talented members of Anahata Chapter of O.T.O. on a filmed presentation of the Mass. At the time of this writing, the video was still available on Vimeo (*https://vimeo.com/gnosticmass/liberxv*) and other streaming platforms; it may be especially useful to those who are unable to attend a Mass in person, or those who are training to serve in the Mass and desire an easy way to review its procedures.

ritual. We can learn a lot from looking at its structure, its flow, and the way its officers embody certain inner principles of every magician. Then, in the second part of the chapter, I'll give suggestions on how you can enhance your own experience of the Mass as an attendee. This will in no sense be an exhaustive study of the breadth and depth of the symbolism of the Mass; nor am I presenting these thoughts in my capacity as an officer of O.T.O., or as "official" doctrine. These are simply my own personal observations and interpretations, drawn from many years of attending the Mass and serving as a Priest and Bishop of Ecclesia Gnostica Catholica (E.G.C.). I encourage you to consider them with your skepticism and critical thinking fully engaged, experiment with my suggestions if you like, and come to your own conclusions.

Part One: Lessons from the Ritual Technology of the Mass

The Gnostic Mass is a lesson in managing our own individual mystical and magical experience. It is a template for executing a personal ritual; an instruction in how to relate to the divine and to the physical world, how to understand one's basic nature, how to harness and direct magical energy, and, quite importantly, how to be of service to the world. Throughout this section, I encourage you to interpret what I say as advice for your own personal work, and not merely as a discussion of the mechanics of an actual Mass. Since I don't want to take space to reprint the entire Mass here, I strongly suggest that you have one of the many published editions of the ritual in front of you as you read this chapter, and of course, consider your own experiences from any Masses you have attended.

Right from the outset, there is a lesson to be drawn from the way the Mass temple is constructed and arranged. You need to have an altar or "shrine" that is sacred to you, and that you treat with respect and even awe. You need a temple setup that somehow symbolizes your "universe." Any magical ritual needs to have a temple space defined in a certain way so as to imply the "field of action" of the magician. So, in the Gnostic Mass temple we have, more or less, a Qabalistic Tree of Life implied by the floor plan. As you likely know, the Tree of Life is a commonly used symbol for the totality of the universe, the inner world of the magician, and the relationship between the two.

Note that only those who plan to communicate are normally present for the Mass. What's the magical instruction here? Obviously, there is the practical matter that you don't want people just wandering in off the street without any intention of participating in the ritual. Interpreted on the inner plane, however, this is a way of saying if there is a part of you that isn't on board with the ritual that you are doing, that is distracted by outer things or isn't committed to the aim of the ritual, don't bring it into the temple with you! Leave that part outside. Compare this general intention with the ritualized equivalent from the Golden Dawn tradition, where an officer proclaims, *Hekas, hekas, este bebeloi* ("Hence, hence ye profane!"), or the opening phrase from the Ritual of the Star Ruby, *apo pantos kakodaimonos* ("Begone, ye evil spirits!").

This brings us to another very important theme we can see developing as the Mass progresses. It involves a traditional sequence of magical steps that can be summarized as: purify, then consecrate, then initiate (see the chapters on Qabalistic psychology and sex magick in *Living Thelema* and the present volume). For one thing, we can consider what happens to the Priest in the West, and the Priestess in the East, as instructions on how to manage the purification, consecration, and initiation of certain parts of ourselves. Purification can be defined in a magical context as "washing away" unwanted elements. When we purify something, typically using magical implements related to water, we wash away those aspects of it that are in the way, or are not aligned with our sacred aims. Next, with consecration, we apply to it the sacred fire to consciously align it with those aims. After the ritual object has been purified and consecrated, we give it a sacred "trajectory" or purpose. That's the "initiation" phase—when something is given its magical aim. You can see this sequence laid out in many traditional examples of consecrations of talismans or magical weapons, and indeed in initiation ceremonies for magicians themselves. (See *The Golden Dawn*,[53] *Magick in Theory and Practice*, and similar resources for much more on this.)

So how do we apply these to the specific actions and tasks of the Priest and Priestess? First of all, we have to decide what aspect of ourselves the Priest represents. One way of thinking about this would be that the Priest is the exemplar of *every human* aspiring to the divine. They are the alchemical first matter, or as the ritual puts it, "a man among men." They are a naturally occurring thing ready to be given a certain mission or aim. When we see the Priest purified by water with the words, "Be the Priest pure of body and soul," we can understand something about how we may prepare ourselves for our own pursuit of the divine. We wash away outer influences, we get rid of our distractions and mundane concerns from the outside world. As at the beginning of any other ritual or endeavor of will, we leave that stuff at the door. With the consecration, the Priestess says, "Be the Priest fervent of body and soul." It's worth noting that while in modern usage the word *fervent* means "having a passionate intensity," the original meaning was more like "hot," "glowing," "burning," "boiling," or "foaming"—which sounds a lot like a consecration by fire to me! The Priest is thereby aligned with and empowered by this "spirit-fire." They are given access to this force only now, after they have been purified. Only then can they be truly initiated into the Priesthood.

What does the Priest *need* for that to occur, and what can this tell us about the nature of their mission? And ours? Some of the necessary tools are represented by key symbols of Thelemic tradition. The Priest needs *solar* force, symbolized by the robe (i.e., "Priest of the Sun"), and *serpent* force, symbolized by the Uraeus crown. These are the empowerments that permit their service to the world. So, we have a purified and

---

[53] Regardie, I. (2015). *The Golden Dawn* (7th ed.). John Michael Greer (Ed.). Woodbury, MN: Llewellyn.

consecrated Priest given the aim of executing a solar/serpentine working. In my view, this reinforces the importance of the spirit-fire and life-power we might call *kundalini*. It is truly the "fuel" of any successful magical working. Residing in *all* humans, it is the real spiritual "phallus" which has so often been misconceived as referring merely to the physical penis. It is channeled from the highest divine sources through the alchemical vessel of the human body; it is stoked by devotion, and directed by the willed intention of the magician toward their desired aims.

Let's now turn our attention to the work of the Priestess. As with the Priest, in order to understand what is happening here, we need to define our vision of what the Priestess represents in terms of our inner life. What does this officer represent within us? It seems to me that they are an exemplar of inner and outer principles of divinity—the idea of divinity itself. If the Priest is the aspirant seeking union with the divine, then the Priestess is that divinity, calling us to such a union. This can be within and without—the divinity that resides within us as well as the divinity that we see in the world all around us; the immanent divinity some have called *shekinah*, or *shakti*, or many other names. Thus, the Priestess is a symbol of the dual nature of spirit, as seen in stories like Wagner's *Parsifal*, where Kundry reveals mysteries of Malkuth as well as Binah. The Priestess is both the immanent divinity in the natural world and the supernal divinity resident above the Abyss. We see that show up in the action of the Mass in terms of the Priestess's coming to the Priest at the tomb of the West as the "Virgin"—the final Heh of the Tetragrammaton (הוהי)—and then being elevated to Binah, embodying the first Heh of the Tetragrammaton.

There is a lesson here on how we may find or recognize spirit in our lives. How do we treat this divine principle within in order to rightly understand it and worship it? The first step is to actually notice it's there, of course. We must recognize it in the world around us, just as the Priest must recognize the Priestess as an emissary and embodiment of the divine and accept their purification, consecration, and initiation as a Priest. To approach the divine in our own lives, we first have to accept its presence and influence in our everyday experience; to recognize it and allow it to imbue us with the necessary principles to engage in our True Will, and in whatever magical aim is before us.

Next, the Priest elevates the Priestess to the highest shrine imaginable, represented by the high altar in the East. What is the lesson here for us as individuals and aspirants? Once we have allowed the divine to do its work on us in the world, then we must try to experience it, understand it, to hold it in a place of inner sanctity so that we can rightly worship it. It is not merely the physical world that we see around us—it *is* that, but it is also much, much more. The purification of the Priestess can be seen as purifying the very idea of the divine, washing away the accretions of limited ideas about divinity and cultural baggage about what God, Goddess, or Divine-Name-of-Your-Choice is supposed to be. It must be purified so that "no alien element intrudes," in order for us to rightly worship it. Then, when the Priest consecrates the Priestess, those purified ideals are aligned with the fiery force of our worship; the fire and force of devotion, passion, and aspiration we give to these spiritual ideals. When the Priestess's initiation is completed—that is, when she is identified with the pentagram and with the Covenant of Resurrection—we can see this as a statement about the true nature of the eternal, undying, divine forces within each of us. So just as the Priest was purified, consecrated, and initiated and given a magical mission to unite with the divine, the Priestess is also purified, consecrated, and initiated, except here the field of operation is our very conception of divinity itself.

Let's look at a few other lessons potentially available to us by studying the structure and formulae of the Mass. As with many rituals, there is a proclamation or an oath, and in this case, it comes in the form of the Creed. This occurs right at the beginning of the ritual, after the temple is appropriately configured and the congregation and officers enter, and it therefore follows the traditional dictum regarding the organization of any magical act: "Thought, then Word, then Deed." To perform an effective magical act, you first have to conceive of it, then you have to speak it forth to give it some momentum, and only then do you physically engage with the magical act. In this instance, the initial setup of the temple is the conceiving Thought, the Creed is the Word, and the rest of the Mass is the Deed.

We also get a lesson in the art of invocation. Consider the Priest's words, "Thee therefore whom we adore we also invoke." This could be read simply as a statement of, "OK, we have adored something and now we are going to invoke it," but there is a deeper teaching here: We invoke something *by* adoring it. The act of adoration aligns us with the very nature of that which is adored, transforming us into a veritable talisman to invite and contain its force. We bring into ourselves some measure of what it is we adore simply through the act of adoring it. There is much to be gained from this principle in our approach to everyday living and spiritual aspiration, not merely in the execution of magical ritual.

At the consecration of the elements, we get a lesson in *how* to consecrate something—anything! Yet, this is a slightly different aspect of consecration than what I discussed earlier. To consecrate something, we have to *name* it, and we see that happening in various ways in the Mass. The Priest's acts embody several layers of this "naming," chiefly by describing the principles that are being consecrated, such as the Host and the wine. Then we have the act of showing the elements to the people. Whenever a ritual officer elevates or performs another gesture with a ritual implement, this is an act of empowering that object with our full consciousness and focused awareness; not just the magician's own, but also that of all those observing, and even (we may surmise) that of the universe itself. So, when the Priest turns and shows the Host and the wine to the people, these objects are truly imbued with more force. Consider this when designing your own rituals.

We also get an instruction in how to treat our inmost shrine of holiness by attending to the way the cup is treated. The veiling and unveiling of the cup are accompanied by gestures of adoration. This is the cup of Babalon, the Holy Grail itself. How do we protect the sanctity of such a magical implement in service of the aim of the ritual? Basically, you don't mess with it unless you are fully mindful of its holiness! You don't unveil the cup unless you are going to do something specific with it that aligns with your magical aim. Then, as soon as you are finished, you veil it again, mindful of what that represents. These acts teach us the right approach to protecting our own shrines and other sacred objects, inner and outer.

We get another instruction in proper invocation from the Anthem, both in terms of the nature of that which we worship and in the specifics of its invocation. As I discussed in the previous chapter, we first identify the "target" of our invocation as more or less an external object, entity, or force. Then, gradually, as seen in the Priest's portion of the Anthem, this changes to a *utilization* of the force being invoked, and finally to a full *identification* with the force. We move from "Thou who art I, beyond all I am . . ." to increasingly possessive and intimate terms like "Thee I invoke, my faint fresh fire . . ." and then, finally, to "that most holy mystery of which the vehicle am I," now fully identified with this force. At this point, we can command or direct it, because we have properly invoked it through such identification with it: "Appear, most awful and most mild, as it is lawful, in thy child!"

As the consummation of the elements is obviously a eucharist, we have here a simple lesson in the execution of a proper eucharist, drawing on all the actions that take place before the consummation. That is: Take an object, use ritual invocations to imbue it with a sacred nature and purpose, and then consume it in order to infuse yourself with that force. "There is no part of me that is not of the Gods." In terms of ritual structure, this is also known as the formation of the so-called "magical link." Alternative approaches to forging this link at the end of a ritual include the conse-cration of a talisman or other magical implement, so that we have access to the force at a later time; and just as this charged magical item is safely wrapped in black silk at the conclusion of the ritual to protect its power, so does the Priest "wrap" themselves in the Tomb of the West at the con-clusion of the Mass, ready to repeat the entire process at the next Mass.

Before that final act, however, we have the Priest's benediction to the people—the final words of the entire Mass. Having partaken of the eucharist, and the people having done the same, all is prepared for this final act of blessing. It could not have occurred earlier, because the forces of the ritual had not yet been dispersed to all present. Since the Priest's magical aim for the Mass was, implicitly, to "administer the virtues to the Brethren," the action of the entire ritual was not complete until everyone had partaken of these virtues and was prepared for this final charge.

Also consider the three lines spoken by the Priest here, in light of the way the Priest themselves was prepared for the work of the Mass:

1. *"The Lord bless you."* The Priest was blessed via their own preparation, purification, consecration, and initiation.

2. *"The Lord enlighten your minds and comfort your hearts and sustain your bodies."* This is a threefold formula of action that corresponds to the threefold manner in which the Priest was prepared by the Priestess, making the three crosses upon them.

3. *"The Lord bring you to the accomplishment of your True Wills, the Great Work, the Summum Bonum, True Wisdom, and Perfect Happiness."* This is what the Priest was empowered do within the ritual itself. We see the Priest enabled to do their True Will (in the context of the Mass) by administering the virtues to the Brethren. The actions, experiences, and transformations that the Priest went through are the very things that empower the people to go forth and do the same via this final benediction. Our lesson: A ritual properly performed empowers the magician to transmit that "virtue" to the outer world, whether that be to other people, to the object being consecrated, or to their outer life in its broadest sense.

One final lesson we can learn from the Mass relates to the principle of *grounding* after a ritual. In the Mass, the Priest consumes the eucharist, administering its virtues to the assembled congregants. At that point the ritual should feel complete, without residual energy uncomfortably present. It's been grounded by virtue of the consumption of the charged eucharist and the shared communion. Magical ritual generates (or at least *should* generate) a lot of force, but we need to be efficient and economical with the use of that force. At the end of the ritual, it should feel as if the force was fully absorbed into the desired intention. So, for example, if you are charging a magical implement of some kind, you want that implement to absorb all of the force and not feel like it's still bouncing around the room when you are done. Without this grounding, those present at a ritual experience agitation, or perhaps feel too "spacey" in the head. This is just the way our everyday consciousness tends to react to that unabsorbed energy floating around. When, on the other hand, the force of a ritual is properly dispersed, you have in a sense "completed a circuit." You have completed your role of bringing that force down from the highest divine levels to the physical world.

These are, of course, only some of the many magical lessons we might distill from the example of the Mass. Your own repeated attendance of the Mass, and your study of its formulae, will undoubtedly suggest many more.

Part Two: Making the Most of Your Experience of the Gnostic Mass

Now that we've reviewed the ritual technology of the Mass, let's take a closer look at some of the ways that you can make your preparation for, and attendance of, the Mass a ritual unto itself. Here you will learn how to choose a magical aim of whatever sort you like, and then approach your whole Mass-going experience as an enactment of that ritual to achieve the aim. Once again, I emphasize that these points are simply my own ideas on the topic, and not necessarily those of O.T.O./E.G.C. as an organization.

The basic assumption here is that everything happening in the Mass is also happening *within* you simultaneously. That is, the actions of each of the Mass officers as well as the overall unfolding of the ritual are enacting a particular process within you, and the more you can tune into it *as* it's happening, the more powerful the ritual may be for you. With such awareness, you will have an opportunity to consciously align the forces unleashed in the Mass with your own True Will, or at least with the magical aim you have chosen, presumably because you believe it to be in harmony with that Will.

Let's start at the beginning. Long before the Mass commences, long before you even get into the car to go to the Mass, you are preparing for it psychologically. You are planning to go and gearing up for the experience. This is a good time to start thinking about what your magical aim will be for the Mass. You can begin this process by taking a cleansing bath, as you might do before any other ritual. Feel this as a washing away of distractions, as a mode of relaxation and an opportunity to focus yourself. Contemplate your desired magical result, and explore any counter-impulses in your mind that might tend to undermine your intention. If a part of you really doesn't want to get the thing that you are saying you want to get, or if you feel guilty about wanting it, you will be less likely to succeed. Similarly, if your outer life circumstances are not conducive to you getting the thing you say you want to get, you will be less likely to succeed. To cite an example I've used before: Don't expect to get a desired new job by just doing a ritual, if you haven't actually put in an application. You need to do the mundane, Malkuth-level behavioral actions that will tend to make your life a hospitable place for the goal to manifest. With all of the above in mind, refine your magical goal accordingly, if necessary. Try to phrase the goal positively, and in a way that consciously connects the desired outcome to the broader "story" of your magical path. That is, it is better to have a goal like "It is my will to have prosperity and ease of circumstances for the performance of the Great Work" rather than "I want to get out of this crappy job."

If you wish, you can then assume a "magical personality" for engaging with the ritual. For example, put on a magical ring, or an article of special ritual clothing, or find some other way of showing (yourself) that you are moving into the realm of conscious magical action, as opposed to the mundane actions of the everyday personality. Then, say to yourself something like "I am Frater/Soror/Sibling [your magical motto], and it is my will to utilize the formulae of this Gnostic Mass to . . ." and fill in the blank with your magical aim.

When you arrive at the temple, be mindful of that moment when you cross its threshold. Try to be as conscious as possible of the distinction between the outside and the inside. You are making this transition inwardly as well, stepping psychologically and spiritually from a place of mundane outer concerns to a place of focused aspiration—fertile spiritual ground for what is about to occur. Resolve at this moment to leave all the distractions and concerns of the outer world behind. Any ego-based desires or fears, things that are clinging to your magical aim and perhaps muddying up your vision of it, must be released now. There will be more ways to do this as the Mass proceeds, of course, but the initial transition through this "liminal" space can be incredibly powerful when conducted mindfully.

After entering the temple, try to stay focused as much as possible on your aim and how that interweaves with the magick and the actions of the Mass. Try not to indulge in idle chatter before the Mass begins. Instead, sit quietly and meditate on your aim. Don't let any part of you that is not aligned with the purpose of the working be in the temple with you.

When you recite the Creed, engage with it as a conscious alignment of yourself with the actions of the Mass. This makes you part of the "battery" of force that makes the Mass work. You, along with the other attendees, are actually in a ritual role, not merely a passive observer. This conscious alignment with the Creed is essentially a variation on the traditional Oath or Proclamation—the implication being that you are engaging with the magick of the Mass to assist with attaining your desired goal.

Watch the actions of the Priest and Priestess in particular. For actions involving the Priest, relate them to your own aspiration to the divine. For actions involving the Priestess, relate them to your own embodiment of the divine; that is, the divine presence within you, however you perceive it. Whether you conceive of this as the relations between an Adept and the HGA, an aspirant and a deity, or something else, one is the motive force—the aspiration, desire, and devotion—and the other is that which is desired, adored, or worshiped.

When the "Virgin" (who is later referred to as the Priestess, of course) enters and says, "Greeting of Earth and Heaven," be aware of the entrance of the divine presence into your consciousness. As they move gently around the small altar and font, feel that divine presence beginning to intermingle with and awaken the physical temple and your physical body. As noted in Part One of this chapter, you might wish to interpret this as the *shekinah*, the immanent deity, that is woven into the fabric of the physical world; the descent of the supernal divine feminine to infuse the physical world and awaken it to the divine presence. With the phrase, "By the power of Iron," feel your aspiration come completely to attention. Remember that iron is symbolically related to Mars, and the "Mars force" is one term for the sexual force, the life force, and the force of will and action, of fire and intensity. Certainly, when you have a magical aim, you want some iron behind it! You must be fully awake in your aspiration. As the Priestess says in their sword-wielding command, you must "Arise"!

In the next phase of the ritual, the Priest is purified, consecrated, and then made a Priest. As noted in Part One, this is a threefold sequence of initiation for both the Priest and the Priestess, but here we'll focus on how this applies to you, your experience of the Mass, and your magical aim.

When the Priestess says, "Be the Priest pure of body and soul," feel your magical aim being cleansed of any accretions or distractions from the outer or inner worlds. The result is that your will, your aim, your aspiration, is left being *nothing but itself*.

With the line "Be the Priest fervent of body and soul," your purified aim is aligned with the spirit-fire and made sacred.

When the Priestess robes the Priest, with the line "Be the flame of the Sun thine ambience, O thou Priest of the Sun," feel yourself glowing with solar force. When they receive the Crown, feel the solar serpent-fire extending up to the crown chakra above your head. Feel yourself as an open channel of this force. As the Priestess strokes the Lance, breathe mindfully from the diaphragm, feeling your entire being open up as a channel for divine force flowing from the highest sources through you, and out to all the universe.

This last action illustrates an important general principle of effective magick, and deserves more discussion. When you identify yourself as a "channel" or "vessel" for the force you are trying to bring through, you are much more likely to succeed. I've seen dozens of magicians get tripped up, burned out, or otherwise psychologically fried if they decide *they* are the source of the required energy. The magician is merely a channel for this infinite, universal force, not its source. Also recognize that when you enact a ritual aim, rightly configuring yourself as a vessel for universal force, and you do so in harmony with True Will, you are serving humanity, since the True Will of an individual is by definition in line with the universal will.

"Thee therefore whom we adore, we also invoke." As discussed in Part One of this chapter, when you adore something inwardly, you call forth that thing to be more present within you. Whatever your magical aim for this ritual experience may be, find a way to *adore* it in connection with the Priestess, and you will thereby *invoke* it. See the Priestess as a symbol of *all* desired outcomes in the universe, and *fall in love* with the beauty of this idea. As the Priest leads the Priestess to the high altar, feel your magical aim itself being elevated to this ultimate place of worship.

Once the Priestess gets to the high altar they go through a similar and parallel purification and consecration as in the earlier "Priest-making" ceremony. While then we experienced the threefold regimen as applying to our own aspiration, here we apply it to the divine itself. In other words, if the Priestess symbolizes our conception of the divine, we want to make sure that conception itself is pure and unpolluted. We want to be sure that what we are holding in our mind as the divine, what we are holding to be worthy of worship, doesn't have alien elements intruding upon it. In my discussions of sex magick, for example, I talk about this as a washing away of Old Aeon conceptions about sexuality, love, and deity. It's not about mindless self-sacrifice. It's not about repressing the body or our sexuality, or demonizing anything connected with the physical world. These are the kinds of ideas that may have stuck onto your own conceptions of the divine, and here is the place to let them be washed away.

Next, the consecration of the Priestess empowers this purified conception of the divine with the spirit-fire. When the veil is closed and the Priest circumambulates, feel this as a feeding of your conception of the divine with the power of silent and secret adoration. You have closed up that most sacred thing behind a veil of secrecy and silence, and whatever is happening back there is happening in its own womb-like space. Identify with the Priest's action as a way of raising the force in that space of silence even further.

When the Priest gives their speech on the first step ("O circle of Stars . . ."), mirror it inwardly as a conscious statement of your conception of the divine that you adore. When the Priest delivers the second speech ("O secret of secrets . . ."), identify with the "Hadit" aspect of yourself which is eternally *experiencing* the divine. The recitation of the calendar can become a conscious alignment of yourself with the Thelemic current in its right celebration, adding the force of community to your personal aims. The Priest's third and final speech on the steps ("Thou that art One . . .") describes the ecstasy available to you in the union of these two prior concepts, the union of divinity itself with the *aspiration* to divinity. This is, of course, one possible summary of what the Mass as a whole is about—the enactment of this union. At the third speech, strive to experience this as your own face-to-face encounter with the divine, under Will. The solar-phallic principle at the root of the Mass is invoked, and empowers your ritual aim. The Priestess then exclaims, "There is no law beyond Do what thou wilt," which you can hear as an affirmation that you are bringing the force of your own Will to the proceedings, and the veil is opened to reveal the shrine once again.

With the recitation of the Collects by the Deacon, you have another opportunity to align your aspiration and your magical aim with the core principles that inform our magick. Indeed, the Collects are in many ways a statement of a complete Thelemic view of the nature of reality, the nature of the four elements and seven principles, and other facts of life such as birth, marriage, and death. The Saints are given as examples of those who have enacted True Will, across the ages, in one way or another. You can experience this as a bit of a pep talk for yourself in terms of enacting whatever your ritual aim may be. (Remember, you should be holding your ritual aim in mind throughout the entire Mass as much as possible, as you also connect with the actions and energies of the ritual.)

During the consecration of the elements—the Host and the wine— imagine that the spiritual "polarities" we've discussed so far (that is, your aspiration to the divine, and the divine itself) are in fact embodied by the Host and the wine. The more power you put into your identification of these two elements, as well as the Lance and the Cup, the more force will be available when these elements (and implements) unite. At the "Covenant of Resurrection" section, and the offering of the elements to "the Sun," offer these elements of yourself to the highest conception of divinity you can imagine. We're approaching the climax here, so your aspiration and your focus on these two elements as they are about to unite should be quite intense by now. (If all of this is starting to turn you on somewhat, you're on the right track!)

The Priest's portion of the Anthem which follows is in fact a very effective "general" invocation—it calls up the undifferentiated spiritual force which is essential for *any* magical operation—so as the Priest is reciting it, feel it as a further ratcheting up the force available to you to flow toward your magical aim. Then, when the antiphony between the "men" and "women" present continues in the Anthem, ride this wave, undulating back and forth between your inner polarities and energizing them to a fever pitch. This energetic building continues through to the climax of the "Mystic Marriage." Be as mindful as possible of your ritual aim as the Lance enters the Cup, and hold this state of mindfulness as completely as you can until you actually consume the Cake of Light and the wine. When you consume them, feel with certainty that they have been charged with your ritual aim. This is a community ritual, but it's also *your* ritual, your experience, and your eucharist. Once again, since it is universal will that empowers our ceremonies, and since your ritual aim has been chosen conscientiously to be aligned with your True Will and therefore this same universal will, you are also performing a service to humanity by consuming this eucharist and completing your ritual. True Will, enacted with Love, is *always* an act of service.

At the closing of the veil, seal up your inner shrine with love, silence, and secrecy. Let this be a final affirmation of the utter holiness of this most dear and divine aspect of your spiritual self. Whatever conceptions you have been able to wrap around the Priestess, seal these up again in your heart, knowing that they are in a sanctified space there.

With the Priest's final words, feel the threefold benediction imparting a blessing on your ritual aim. Imagine that the Priest, who has been acting as a symbol of your own aspiration to the divine and your own enactment of your ritual aim, is turning to you and saying, with the voice of the universe itself, "Your ritual was successful, your desired result will be obtained, your aim has been sanctified, and your prayers have been heard by the gods" (or however you prefer to think of the divine). In any case, let this be a moment where you feel a final sense of absolute certainty that your ritual is complete, and your goal is attained.

CHAPTER 11

THE GOLDEN DAWN TRADITION IN MODERN THELEMA

POST CXX ANNOS PATEBO[54]

Aleister Crowley had his first ceremonial initiation experience when he became a Neophyte of the Hermetic Order of the Golden Dawn (HOGD) in 1898—a date he later regarded as his true "magical birthday." In the 135 years that have passed since its founding in 1888,[55] the Golden Dawn and its various offshoots have proven themselves to be among the most influential traditions within ceremonial magick and occultism generally. Yet in parallel with this, something of a philosophical schism has emerged in the way many modern occultists tend to think about the relationship between Thelema and its HOGD-patterned contemporaries. I've noticed that many Thelemites tend to downplay the importance of the Golden Dawn system, likely due to Crowley's occasionally

---

[54] From the Hermetic Order of the Golden Dawn's Adeptus Minor initiation, and typically rendered as, "At the end of 120 years, I, the light of the cross, will disclose myself." See Regardie, I. (2015). *The Golden Dawn* (7th ed.). John Michael Greer (Ed.). Woodbury, MN: Llewellyn.

disparaging remarks, and an apparent conclusion that all such "Old Aeon" orders have nothing to teach us in this age of Thelema. I've also noticed that many Golden Dawn–rooted magicians similarly look down upon Crowley and his teachings, perhaps due to a certain squeamishness about Crowley's reputation in the occult world. In this chapter, I will argue that there is quite a lot to be learned from Golden Dawn–patterned systems in the New Aeon, whether one initially approaches them with Thelemic or non-Thelemic sympathies.

To begin this discussion, it is necessary to define what we even mean (in today's world) when we refer to a Golden Dawn–patterned order. After all, there have been many offshoots, splinters, modifications, and elaborations of the original order, and that can pose a challenge when attempting to pin down the basic nature of the system. The original HOGD had a framework of rituals and teachings based on what were called the *cypher manuscripts*. These manuscripts were either written or "discovered," depending on who you believe, by the founders of the HOGD; they contain skeletal outlines of rituals that were developed later into the actual functioning rituals of the order. Its initiatory degrees or grades were based on the Qabalistic Tree of Life, with each grade relating to one of the sephiroth of the Tree of Life. The experience of going through a grade ritual—its tone and its teachings, and the work that the initiate was to undertake during their time in the grade—was designed to stimulate and instruct both the conscious as well as the unconscious mind. The idea was that certain symbol sets would be impressed upon the mind in specific ways, gradually building an internal "map" for the spiritual growth of the initiate. It was a very powerful way of getting a thorough "from the ground up" instruction in Qabalah, basic correspondences (such as one finds in Crowley's *777*), the Hebrew alphabet, and similar building blocks of artful ceremonial magick.

---

[55] Exactly 120 years before the founding of Temple of the Silver Star.

In 1900, not long after Crowley's initiation into the HOGD, a schism occurred. Crowley, for a while, was loyal to S. L. M. Mathers (one of the order's founders), but eventually he left the order. His experience in the Golden Dawn was negatively colored by his professed distaste for its social politics, and the jockeying for grades and personal power that reportedly occurred in its ranks. His perception was that advancement was being awarded to people based largely on their wealth or social standing. (We will save a discussion of Crowley's potential psychological projections in this regard for another occasion.) He also felt that the instructions in the HOGD's Outer Order were too basic, and he was anxious to make the whole process of initiation and training more efficient. In any case, he went on to publish the order's rituals in *The Equinox*, while simultaneously disparaging its social approach and many of its members. His experiences in the HOGD prompted him to found his own Tree of Life–based system of instruction known as A∴A∴. Unfortunately, in his haste to strip out what he deemed to be rather basic preparatory materials, he underestimated the value this foundational training might have for future students, probably due in part to his own capacity for acquiring and integrating occult knowledge so quickly.

In formulating the system of A∴A∴, Crowley more or less tossed aspirants into the equivalent of the Second Order HOGD experience, right from the beginning. He was ready to let aspirants sink or swim; to come in with a minimum of background, study intensely, and pursue an essentially self-paced course of study with a single instructor. With all due respect to the incredible work that Crowley did in structuring A∴A∴, I think he did remove something of value that many students have subsequently found important. In my teaching capacity in various Thelemic orders over the years, I have noticed that when aspirants to A∴A∴ have had the opportunity to go through some sort of structured preparatory training, when they have internalized the basic meanings of the paths and the sephiroth on the Tree of Life and truly integrated them, they hit the ground running in A∴A∴. They have already done the basic memorization tasks, they have had the benefit of working with daily rituals and keeping a magical diary, and they have moved through an initiatory system that mirrors, albeit at a lower level of intensity, that of A∴A∴. Not every aspirant needs such preparatory work in order to succeed in A∴A∴, but I have found that *many* certainly benefit from it.

Let's review how we can take the best of what exists in the basic Golden Dawn framework—the "landmarks" of the Golden Dawn system, if you will—and bring them into a Thelemic context. I'll be discussing this mostly from the standpoint of the Thelemic Golden Dawn–patterned order I administer, the Temple of the Silver Star (TOTSS), because that's what I'm most intimately familiar with, but these principles would potentially apply to any group attempting to fuse these two traditions. Seeing Thelema as an elaboration and an expansion of the Golden Dawn, instead of something that entirely replaces it, brings several advantages. It provides the preparatory training discussed earlier, yet it also allows for a more nuanced understanding of the paths and the sephiroth in the context of their Thelemic import. How might we update the traditional Golden Dawn curriculum to be workable in a Thelemic context and to make sense in the New Aeon?

Firstly, the "Old Aeon" Golden Dawn implementation brought candidates to a climactic identification with Osiris as the initiator. The godform of Osiris was the symbolic initiator, and the central archetype of the perfected initiate with which candidates were supposed to identify. In the TOTSS system, the aspirant is symbolically "Osiris" right from the beginning, before their initiation even begins. They walk in the door identified with Osiris, so our system is essentially bringing one candidate at a time into the New Aeon via the initiation ritual. As Thelemites, we have moved on to the New Aeon, and rather than having Osiris as our main point of identification, we have Horus. We read in *The Book of the Law*, "Ra-Hoor-Khuit hath taken his seat in the East at the Equinox of the Gods, Hoor and his secret name and splendor is the Lord Initiating."[56] This doesn't make too much sense until you recognize that we now have Ra-Hoor-Khuit taking his seat as the enthroned Hierophant in our reconfigured Thelemic temple, as the new symbol of the perfected initiate, and the initiating officer.

Secondly, in the Old Aeon, there was a great deal of emphasis on the so-called LVX formula in connection with the "Dying God" archetype. This showed up in the traditional Golden Dawn system as a focus on the initiator/god as an external redeemer, clearly influenced by the dominant Christ-myth of the last 2000 years. In TOTSS, we have removed that emphasis and put the focus where we think it rightly belongs—we Thelemites redeem *ourselves*, dying and being reborn in every moment of life as the child-consciousness of *The Book of the Law*.[57]

As we would hope and expect, the rituals in TOTSS have themselves been transformed from their original Golden Dawn roots. We have had the benefit of several predecessor orders across the last century to help us with this, because we are an unbroken, living tradition. The rituals have been updated to be entirely in accord with the Thelemic dispensation, so we have the concept of True Will as the central guiding principle. We have recast the ordeals and the mysteries connected with the sephiroth and the paths, as well as the tasks, the rituals themselves, and the individual work of each initiate, to be in accord with the Law of Thelema. We have also continued the process of removing sexist language and doctrines, and benefit from more than a century of advances in modern psychology. Most particularly, the work of Jung, Assagioli, and others has brought us powerful transformational technologies that were simply not available at the time the original Golden Dawn, or even in Crowley's lifetime. In TOTSS in particular we benefit from a connection to my own

---

[56] In Crowley, A. (1997). *Magick: Liber ABA* (2nd rev. ed.). Hymenaeus Beta (Ed.). York Beach, ME: Red Wheel/Weiser, LLC, 307.

[57] See Chapter 2 of the present volume.

teacher, Soror Meral (Phyllis Seckler), who placed a strong emphasis in her teaching on psychological balance, self-knowledge, and the importance of approaching magical work from the standpoint of a healthy human personality that isn't blind to its own ego drives and impulses.

So why would you want to do this sort of work? If you want "from the ground up" training in Qabalah, tarot, astrology, ceremonial magick, and meditation, this is a structured way to get it. If you want progressive instruction on Thelemic philosophy, with a specific focus on the discovery of the True Will, you'll find it here as well. As an example of the centrality of the True Will to our training system in TOTSS, no one moves from our First Order into our Second Order until they are able to articulate an understanding of their True Will in a single phrase. That doesn't mean it will be an unchanging conception for them forever, but until they are able to put it into words based on several years of in-depth personal and magical work, they won't progress beyond First Order mysteries. The Second Order of TOTSS, initiated by the attainment of our Tiphareth degree, does not constitute full K&C of the HGA as it would for an Adeptus Minor of A∴A∴—but it must involve a new breakthrough of awareness concerning the spiritual purpose of the initiate, and the TOTSS system is full of magical as well as psychological training for this breakthrough.

We teach specific tools for building the ability to generate and channel magical force—a magical and ritual "technology" that has been developed over millennia, and in terms of our immediate predecessor orders, over the course of more than a century, with each successive order adding its own flavor, tools, and personality. Even experienced magicians may find that the structure and tools we present in TOTSS bring a new level of self-awareness, and a new dimension of understanding to Thelemic and Qabalistic concepts.

Another benefit of the work in TOTSS that is important to some (but not necessarily all) aspirants is that we actually are a lineal descendent of the original Golden Dawn. We are a link in an unbroken chain of successor orders of the Golden Dawn; a chain where at each new iteration advanced initiates from the Second Order have branched off to form an entirely new order. This isn't a situation where someone picked up Regardie's book *The Golden Dawn* and decided to start an order; in TOTSS, we are following more than a century of unbroken, living tradition, Hierophant to Hierophant, initiator to initiator, from Mathers to the present.

Finally, another reason that people might want to pursue this work with TOTSS specifically is our linkage to A∴A∴. We are "in service to A∴A∴," and as I mentioned earlier, many people who have had preliminary training in TOTSS have gone on to great success in A∴A∴ because of that running start. Let me emphasize that by joining TOTSS, one doesn't join A∴A∴. They are separate orders, and membership in one does not constitute or require membership in the other. A∴A∴ functions on its own plane, in accordance with the landmarks originally established by Crowley and G. C. Jones, and there is absolutely no requirement or expectation that people go through the TOTSS system in order to enter A∴A∴.

One's work in groups like TOTSS is greatly enhanced by the ability to participate in a recurring monthly ritual, which has an emphasis on energy raising, healing, and magical instruction. There is an unquestionable benefit to doing regular work of this sort, refining your ability to move energy, embody god-forms, and develop skills in the very subtle aspects of conducting effective magical work. There is simply no replacement for doing this on a regular basis alongside other like-minded and committed initiates.

I have told you quite a lot about the Temple of the Silver Star specifically here, and of course I want people to know about it, but my primary aim has been to show that the underlying system of the Golden Dawn has much to offer within the context of Thelemic philosophy and practice. It is hardly a worn-out Old Aeon husk—rather, it is a well-defined and superbly structured system that can form the foundation of our continuing evolution in the New Aeon.

CHAPTER 12

HEALING

Most of my writing, lecturing, and teaching in magick has, perhaps not unexpectedly, focused on the psychological and spiritual dimensions of life. In this chapter, however, I'll turn my attention to the physical health of the magician, and the practices that can potentially enhance it. Let's begin by reviewing some of Crowley's comments on the nature of physical health, drawn from his essay, "The Elixir of Life."

> As in philosophy, change is life, stagnation death; we should not fear a brisk metabolism. Why should the process which we [called] growth only a few years ago become degeneration? For the same reason that a well-kept, well-oiled machine works more easily with age while a rusty one wrecks itself. Exercise helps us to sluice our sewers, but we must flush them well with water to dissolve mineral waste. We must avoid the ingestion of foods likely to leave insoluble deposits.

> But there is another cause of decay, cause also in part of this poisoning. Our organs would repair themselves perfectly, if they were given sufficient rest. In their haste they absorb the first material to hand, be it good or bad. Also, we call on

them to work before they are fully rested and so we wear them
gradually out. Exercise is necessary to keep us clean; but our
rest must be perfect restoration also. We can give the muscles
this benefit by Asana, and also thereby reduce to a minimum
the work of heart and lungs. We can give our digestion rest
by eating only at noon and sunset, thus allowing them a clear
twelve hours of the twenty-four. Pranayama is the ideal exer-
cise, as it promotes metabolism to the utmost with the mini-
mum of fatigue, and can be combined with Asana. . . .

The man with the best chance of prolonged youth is he who eats
and drinks heartily, not caring what, who does things vigor-
ously in the open air, with the minimum of common-sense pre-
cautions, and who keeps his mind at the same time thoroughly
active, free from worry, and his heart high. He has come, with
William Blake, to the Palace of Wisdom by the Road of Excess.
He is on friendly terms with Nature, and though he does not
fear her, he heeds her, and does not provoke her. "It is better,"
says he, "to wear out than to rust out." True, but is there need
to wear out? He tires himself improperly, and he digs his grave
with his own teeth.[58]

While we might not want to take everything Crowley says here as a
substitute for professional medical advice and common-sense personal
research, this does give us a glimpse of his general conception of the nature
of physical health and those practices and attitudes toward living that, in
his mind, would tend to sustain us and promote our health. Theories of
magick, or attitudes toward the body which are informed by such theories, should not replace professional medical care. If you are ill, please do
seek out professional help, but *also* consider all the techniques I present in

---

[58] Crowley, A. (1990). *Amrita: Essays in Magical Rejuvenation.* Martin P. Starr (Ed.). Kings
Beach, CA: Thelema Publications, 21–3.

this chapter. I also want to second Crowley's implication throughout the previous passage that underlying general physical health is of the utmost importance. You cannot expect to use conventional medical means or magical means to heal yourself from an illness if you are not paying attention to basic daily common sense in terms of the upkeep of your body. Over the decades I've been involved with Thelema, I have watched many individuals utilize the practices in our system of magick and yoga. Their efforts were clearly working—until they undermined them with detrimental behaviors such as excessive use of drugs or alcohol, or simply ignoring common sense in terms of nutrition and exercise. So, perhaps they ended up about where they would have been without the magick!

What magical practices might aid us in caring for our health? Let's start with the importance of daily banishing rituals, as described in detail in *Living Thelema*. These practices really do seem to promote a sort of magical "hygiene," but it's also the sort of hygiene that seems to bring with it enhanced physical health for many practitioners. This is equally true of the yoga practices, as I noted above. Now, we don't really have controlled, scientific studies on the health of people who perform daily banishings compared to those who don't—perhaps that's something we can do in the future. Nevertheless, cumulative anecdotal evidence in my own practice and in observing people across the years suggests that when you are cleansing yourself magically, your body tends to respond to that and benefit. (In case you haven't already heard enough of me recommending that you keep up with your daily rituals, here is another dose of finger-wagging in that direction.)

The use of the invoking rituals on a daily basis can also, in my experience, be a source of healing force. For example, you can simply direct the force from the invoking forms of the pentagram and hexagram rituals you are already doing daily to the healing of the body. This is probably one of the simplest magical or ritual techniques available for such a purpose.

There are advanced healing procedures taught within a number of traditions, including the Second Order of the Temple of the Silver Star.

These often involve the combination of ritual techniques with the targeted use of specific invocations, and the systematic application of color and sound. It is also widely known that Crowley believed the core magical techniques taught in O.T.O. and elsewhere could be applied to curative ends. Again from "The Elixir of Life":

> We know a vehicle of which a few grains can house enough pure Life to fill a man not only with nourishment, but with Energy almost superhuman, and parallel, intelligence incredibly sunbright for four-and-twenty hours. That substance is theoretically easy, but practically hard, to obtain. . . . We know how to charge this substance with the Life-force. . . . We cannot understand the true Nature of this force; we cannot measure it; we cannot create it, or obtain it synthetically.

> But we can purify and intensify it, we can, within wide limits, determine at will the quantity and scope of its action; we can postpone death, increase energy or prolong youth; and we are justified in saying that we possess the Elixir of Life.[59]

I encourage you to contemplate these comments in light of the chapter of *Living Thelema* concerning sex magick, and the material on Qabalistic psychology in the present volume.

As Crowley might agree, change is life, and stagnation is death. Any practice that circulates energy in the physical body or in the aura (or the Body of Light, or any other term of your choosing) will tend to be health-promoting. Let's look at one such exercise, which I offer for your experimentation. This is a modified Middle Pillar exercise where the aim is to focus on certain physical and energetic centers of the body, and "bring down" vital life force from the crown to the heart to the genitals

---

[59] Crowley, A. (1990). *Amrita: Essays in Magical Rejuvenation*. Martin P. Starr (Ed.). Kings Beach, CA: Thelema Publications, 26–7.

and to the feet. The idea is to allow the nature of these different centers of the body to express themselves and enhance the force as we bring it down; to bring their own particular nature and power to the force in service of healing. We see Kether at the crown center, above the head, as the ultimate source of healing force—the divine light and source of life itself. At Tiphareth, the heart, we unite the healing force with the idea of the Holy Guardian Angel, with the intention that the healing is being provided for the furtherance of our own Great Work. In this sense, we might think of the HGA as the healing force as it specifically applies to each individual person. At Yesod, the genitals, we conceptualize that our own regenerative power, our own *personal* creative force, is brought into play to further fuel this healing. Finally, as we bring the light down to the feet, standing on the earth at the Malkuth center, we formulate the awareness that everything that has gone before is now locking itself into the physical body, much like we are charging our body itself as a talisman of that healing force. Finally, we perform a circulation of the force around the perimeter of the aura, down the front and up the back several times.

Exercise

1. Stand in a balanced posture, hands at your sides, feet comfortably close together, with the insides touching or almost touching.

2. Begin to regularize your breathing. With each exhalation, allow the muscles of your body to grow warmer, looser, and more relaxed.

3. Visualize the aura as a vibrant "egg" of blue/white light extending about a foot above your head, a foot below your feet, and a foot outward on all sides of your body. The visualization should be so sharp and solid that it feels like you could reach out and tap on it. All the visualizations of the centers of the body will be within this egg and not touching it.

4. Above your head, see a sphere of brilliant, white light; this is the crown center of Kether. Feel this ultimate source of life and healing; it is vibrant and alive, intense with force, and ready to manifest itself for this healing purpose. When you have this idea locked firmly in mind, vibrate the divine name *Eheieh* (היהא, pronounced EH-HEH-YEH) one time.

5. See a column of white light descend from the crown center to a point at the heart, where it grows to another sphere of white light. This force from Kether is now filling the heart center. Know with certainty your Holy Guardian Angel is ever-present within you, supporting all that you do along your path. When this idea is firmly in your mind, and the healing light has taken on the linkage to your own HGA, vibrate the divine name *IAO* (יאו, pronounced EE-AHH-OH) one time.[60]

6. See a column of white light descend from the heart center to a point at the genitals, where it grows into another sphere of white light. With this, the force of the HGA is now united with your own inherent, divine regenerative power; your own personal healing light mingles with what you have brought down, and this further fuels and enlivens the healing force available to you. When this idea is firmly conceived, vibrate the divine name *Shaddai El Chai* (יח לא ידש, pronounced SHA-DYE-EE ĀLE KYE-EE) one time.

7. With all that has gone before fully formulated and ready to manifest for the furtherance of your own Great Work through the healing of your body, see the column of light descend to a point centered between the feet, where it grows into another

---

[60] IAO is a Gnostic exclamation of ecstasy, but notably it is also a *notariqon* of the traditional divine name of Tiphereth, *YHVH Eloah V'Da-ath* (*tadw hwla hwhy*).

sphere of white light half above and half below the floor. Know as you see this occur that the healing light is now infusing the entirety of your body. As you continue to breathe, feel this force interpenetrating all the cells of your body. See and feel the column of light spreading out throughout your body, and filling the space between your body and the outer edges of the aura. When this idea is firmly conceived, vibrate the divine name *Adonai Ha-Aretz* (צרא ה ינדא, pronounced AH-DOH-NYE HA-ARETZ) one time.

8. Feeling the column connecting the centers firmly established within the egg-like aura, on your next inhalation draw the light up the back of the aura from the feet to the crown; then, on the exhalation see it move down the front of the aura back to the feet. Continue this circulation for three to five breath cycles.

9. Having completed the exercise and circulated the force, you may direct the force to any particular areas of the body you feel need specific healing, or simply see it permeating and benefiting your entire body. Regardless of your choice here, spend a few moments immersed in the light, absorbing its health-enhancing influence.

10. Allow the visualizations to fade, knowing that the powers and potencies you have invoked remain vibrant and active in you.

11. Give the Sign of Silence (the right forefinger placed on the lips) to signal that the exercise is completed.

Additional Notes on the Middle Pillar Exercise

In addition to the healing focus of the adapted version given above, the Middle Pillar exercise can be used daily as a part of your ongoing magical regimen. (When used for this daily "hygienic" purpose, I suggest vibrating the names at each center *three* times instead of just one, and using the Qabalistic Cross from the Lesser Ritual of the Pentagram rather than merely the circulation of energy as in the version above.) I suggest adding the Middle Pillar exercise to your daily practice as an additional "power-up" component, after at least several months of work with the Lesser Banishing and Invoking Rituals of the Pentagram. Then, after adding the Lesser Rituals of the Hexagram and working with them for a few months, you might consider changing to the Queen Scale[61] color attributions of the various centers:

Crown: White brilliance

Throat: Slightly less brilliant white, almost gray

Heart: Yellow-gold

Genitals: Violet

Feet: Olive (my color preference from among the "Malkuth" colors for this particular ritual purpose, for various technical reasons)

The theory is that moving from white light to color will amp up the flow of the current. You might even employ the King Scale colors eventually and occasionally, but only after many months (or even years) of practice with the white-light and Queen Scale versions. In my experience, these changes in color scale can and do make a significant difference in the available energy, and it is not wise to get ahead of yourself in this regard. As with all magical training, a gradual and progressive building of your energy tolerance is essential.

The Middle Pillar may also be employed as a general invocation as a part of a larger ritual. It has all the necessary characteristics for such a purpose, most importantly the ability to generate generic magical force which can then be directed to specific ends via additional invocations or sub-rituals (see the chapter on methods of ritual construction in *Living*

---

[61] See Crowley, A. (2005). *777 and Other Qabalistic Writings of Aleister Crowley*. York Beach, ME: Red Wheel/Weiser, LLC..

Thelema). The exercise may also be used to enhance astral explorations and scrying. Once you have externalized your Body of Light and transferred consciousness to it, you can perform the Middle Pillar *in* your Body of Light as a way of bringing more force to that astral form.

Regarding the technique of the vibrations: Take in a full breath through the nose, and use the entire exhalation for the vibrated names. Place approximately equal emphasis on each letter of the name you are vibrating; a slight elongation of the final letter may occur naturally. Shorter names, such as IAO, will result in each letter receiving a greater proportion of the total exhalation and sound "slower," whereas longer names, such as Shaddai el Chai, will sound as if they are paced more quickly, with less time spent on each letter. Extended practice will teach you what you need to know for your own maximum benefit.

CHAPTER 13

FINDING A TEACHER AND FINDING A SCHOOL

Over the years, many aspirants have written to me asking for advice on finding a good magical teacher, or a legitimate and competent school for their magical training. Furthermore, as an administrator of several magical orders, it's something that is obviously on my mind quite frequently. My daily routine nearly always includes some aspect of instruction or supervision—reviewing diaries or other assignments, meeting with students to train them on ritual technique, or conducting training sessions for those who are themselves teachers in the orders I administer. In this chapter, I'll give suggestions on what to look for, what to avoid, and what questions to ask when considering a potential teacher or school.

I'd like to begin by reading from *Liber Causae*, which is a foundational document of Crowley's magical order, known as A∴A∴:

> 1. In the beginning was Initiation. The flesh profiteth nothing;
> the mind profiteth nothing; that which is unknown to you
> and above these, while firmly based upon their equilibrium,
> giveth life.

2. In all systems of religion is to be found a system of Initiation, which may be defined as the process by which a man comes to learn that unknown Crown.

3. Though none can communicate either the knowledge or the power to achieve this, which we may call the Great Work, it is yet possible for initiates to guide others.

4. Every man must overcome his own obstacles, expose his own illusions. Yet others may assist him to do both, and they may enable him altogether to avoid many of the false paths, leading no whither, which tempt the weary feet of the uninitiated pilgrim. They can further insure that he is duly tried and tested, for there are many who think themselves to be Masters who have not even begun to tread the Way of Service that leads thereto.[62]

This passage, especially the fourth line, serves to underpin one of my central points: Not everyone "needs" a teacher to attain, but just about everyone can be helped by one somehow. I should begin by emphasizing that we learn from all kinds of people, via all kinds of experiences, all the time. We should approach life with an openness, willingness, and even an *eagerness* to learn from everyone we encounter. We learn from our children, our friends, our spouses, our parents, and of course from our actual teachers in school. So in this broad sense, teachers are around us all the time, waiting for us to pay attention—but that's not the sort of teacher I am addressing in this chapter. Here, I'm talking about finding a formal teacher within a Thelemic organization that is focused on training and testing on specific skills in magick and mysticism.

As you may know, I have been involved in Ordo Templi Orientis for decades, and I have found a great deal of value in its system, as have many other aspirants. Some have said over the years that O.T.O. is not a teaching

---

[62] Crowley, A. (1983). *The Equinox*, Vol. III, No. 9. York Beach, ME: Weiser, xxxix.

order, but I disagree; it is a powerful system with important lessons. Its teachings are communicated though initiation rituals, classes, and exposure to the mysteries of *Liber XV*, The Gnostic Mass. It is not, however, a teaching and testing order in the same sense as A∴A∴, or Golden Dawn–derived orders like TOTSS. You don't have an assigned teacher in O.T.O.; there is no one other than yourself who is directly responsible for guiding your *personal* spiritual progress in the traditional sense. Additionally, progress in its system is not generally dependent on the application of specific ritual skills, memorization of correspondences, demonstrated competence with specific aspects of *asana*, *dharana*, or *pranayama*, and so on, as one finds in A∴A∴ and elsewhere. For these reasons, as valuable as O.T.O. is as a teaching system, it's not the *type* of system I am focusing on in this chapter.

The essential characteristic of a true magical training order, or "mystery school," is that the tools of magick and mysticism are rigorously taught and tested, from the foundations all the way through to advanced practices. In other words, it really is a *school*. Now, as you may have noticed, some magicians have issues with authority; but schools have teachers, and schools teach specific approaches to the contents of their curricula. If you want to learn without a teacher, or if you want to learn in a way that doesn't follow along with a certain traditional approach or line of instruction in a given school, *then don't apply to that school*! I am mystified by people who join an organization, but want to do it "their way." Imagine applying to any other sort of school that teaches specific techniques, paying the fees, showing up for class, receiving a textbook, and then announcing that you're going to stay in the school, but ignore their lessons and instead do the work however strikes your fancy. You likely wouldn't waste your time doing that; you simply wouldn't apply to that school.

Having covered these preliminaries, let's review some of the things you may want to consider when evaluating a potential teacher:

1. Did they themselves have a formal teacher in the tradition within which they are purporting to teach? In other words, if they are

portraying themselves as an expert in a particular approach, who did they learn it from? Self-instruction and self-study are incredibly important, but you are not really a teacher in a tradition if you haven't been instructed by someone *in that tradition*. They should be able to tell you the name (at least the magical motto, if not the civil name) of their teacher, or line of teachers.

2. Did the prospective teacher's own teacher review their work specifically? Were their diaries submitted to and read by their teacher? Did that teacher evaluate their ritual performance and test them in ways they couldn't have tested themselves? That's one of the advantages of training in a school of this type: There are certain things you just can't effectively test yourself on, but as Crowley states in *Liber Causae*, it is possible for initiates to guide others, and to help them avoid some of the pitfalls and blind spots that often result from purely solitary study.

3. How long have they been teaching? How long have they been taking students? Those are two different questions altogether. You'll find many people who have been teaching a class here and there since their early adulthood, but how long have they actually been taking on one-to-one personal students in the tradition they claim to be operating in?

4. Do they have enough life experience to effectively teach you? By experience I don't just mean chronological age, although that can certainly bring its own brand of wisdom. I'm referring to the sort of broad and deep life experience that can inform their teaching, bringing with it an emotional and intellectual maturity. If you feel that you are more emotionally and intellectually mature than the person you are considering as a teacher, you are less likely to benefit from that relationship. Furthermore, if someone simply *comes across* as emotionally or intellectually immature, that's a

bright red flag about their personal level of spiritual attainment, and therefore their credibility as a teacher.

5. Are they a good match with you, personality-wise? Would you want to hang out with this person socially? Would you want them in your house? Are you comfortable with them, or do they creep you out? Pay attention to your brain, your heart, and your intuition, and don't ignore red flags. I understand that magical training is not a place you go for comfort. This stuff is hard. Being rigorously tested on certain practices, being corrected or required to repeat tests, can be challenging and frustrating; but you shouldn't be interpersonally uncomfortable with a prospective teacher. If you are getting that uneasy feeling in your stomach, if the person is just a little too creepy, or if you just don't see yourself really *relaxing* into a teacher/student relationship with them, you may want to look elsewhere.

Now let's review things to look for in a potential school or magical order. Some of these points may be fairly obvious, and others perhaps not:

1. How are the teaching and training accomplished? What are the methods? At Golden Dawn–patterned orders like the Temple of the Silver Star, for example, teaching and training are accomplished through regular attendance at group rituals, individual daily practices, keeping a diary, and submitting that diary for evaluation. You'll want to ask about the specifics of how you will be trained. Ask who will be reviewing your magical diary or have access to it, and how its security is safeguarded. What is the confidentiality policy concerning material in the diary? Are diaries kept permanently, or are they returned? (For the record, TOTSS never keeps members' diaries.)

2. How is testing accomplished? Again using TOTSS as a reference point, we test students formally on their performance of

individual rituals, and on their knowledge base through written tests and reports. We also test them informally by observing their ritual performance, how they carry themselves, and the subtle qualities of their energetic work in ritual. Similarly, in A∴A∴, there are well-documented tests built into the system. For example, in the Neophyte grade, the initiate is working on building their competence with the Body of Light (the astral body), astral projection, and scrying, so there are certain tests put in place to make sure they are gaining competence in these skills. No one advances to the next grade until they have demonstrated competence; you simply *can't* move through the system without gaining these competencies. If someone is in fact a Zelator in a legitimate A∴A∴ claimant group, you can be assured that they are competent in their work with the Body of Light, since they will have passed that series of tests as a Neophyte. Thus, in true testing and training orders, *grades actually mean something* about a person's attainment; they are not simply badges they get to wear because they have hung around long enough, or have paid a fee to advance. I cannot overemphasize the importance of this point.

3. What tradition is the school following? Does it have a clearly documented and unbroken connection to Crowley, as is the case in A∴A∴, or (if applicable) to the Hermetic Order of the Golden Dawn or similar organizations? These historical connections aren't necessarily important to everyone when they are looking for a magical order or a teacher; but again, if you're bothering to pursue work within a given tradition, you have to make sure the school is legitimately carrying on that tradition, and not simply *saying* it does. It should be able to provide some form of clear documentation of teacher-to-student relationships extending back to the founders of the tradition. In A∴A∴, for example, we give every new Probationer documentation for *all* the teachers in

their line, extending back to Crowley. Likewise, in the Temple of the Silver Star, we trace our heritage back through a number of predecessor orders, extending in an unbroken, always-active line to the Hermetic Order of the Golden Dawn, via Mathers's original Alpha et Omega. Our ordained Hierophants embody a chain of personal initiatory contact back to Mathers himself. If these historical connections are important to you, be sure to do your research and know what you are getting into. On the other hand, there are plenty of people who don't care about such things, and are content to work outside of any historical or traditional connections. That's just fine with me; as I discussed above, life itself brings us teachers of all kinds—but it's a different sort of training.

There are certain advantages to having a tradition actively worked, enhanced, and revised over many decades or longer— truly a *living* tradition. Legitimate magical orders that have functioned unceasingly over this sort of time span can incorporate advances in magical practice, physical science, psychology. They can work continually to remove the residue of sexism, racism, and "Old Aeon" baggage from the system. When you have hundreds of initiates actively working in a living system over the course of decades, plugged into the "current," it brings a wholly unique training experience. There is a momentum, a spiritual momentum of sorts, that simply isn't there for a "start-up" order. That is not to denigrate newly sprouted groups; in fact, we could probably make the argument that such orders are more likely to avoid the pitfalls of inflexible tradition. This is inevitably a case-by-case consideration.

There are many other lines of inquiry you might want to consider as well. For example, what happens at the meetings of the organization? Does it involve group ritual, or does it consist only of classes? Is attendance at meetings required? How often do they occur? Are there dues? If so, where does that money go? Are there salaried clergy or employees, or is the order composed solely of volunteers? Is it a recognized non-profit organization? What is its structure or hierarchy? If you get the sense that the representatives of the group you are investigating are not willing to talk or interested in talking about these details, that itself is a red flag. There should be a *reasonable* degree of transparency here. If you get a chance, talk to rank and file members of the organization, not just to its leaders. Attend public meetings or ceremonies, if possible, and try to get a sense of the "tone" of these meetings. Do the members seem well adjusted? Do they seem like people you would like to hang around with? If you would feel uncomfortable having these potential "siblings" in your home, then why would you want to enter into a ritual experience with them? It's pretty basic human relations stuff! You want to feel comfortable. You want to feel like these are healthy people that you are spending time with. Do their outer lives suggest an ability to manage life on Earth, not just navigate arcane tomes?

Now for the hard part. Remember, you are potentially joining a magical order. It's a privilege, not a right. The teachers and administrators know what is in their system; you don't. Some practices, such as those of the original Golden Dawn and of A∴A∴. have been published, but you still don't know how a particular group might be implementing them. And you don't know what revisions or enhancements might have crept into the group even if the basic material *is* published. In any case, the final authority on an organization is going to be the leadership of that organization. They will have a better sense of whether *their* system is likely to be a good fit for you than you do. Don't take it personally if you are not accepted for admission. It's very likely to be an issue of matching of the student to the system. There may be many other groups that are a better fit for you.

CHAPTER 14

THE KNOWLEDGE AND CONVERSATION OF THE HOLY GUARDIAN ANGEL: A PERSONAL MEMOIR

Over the past two decades or so, I have spoken quite a bit about the experience of Knowledge and Conversation of the Holy Guardian Angel, but almost always in general terms. Occasionally, I have added a few reflections about my own experience, but always in a supplementary manner. In recent months, however, I've been feeling an increasing impulse to speak in much more detail about my experience, which occurred in December 2004, in the hopes that it may be useful to others walking the path. I've had some hesitance about doing this, to be honest. It is so personal, and so intimate. The years immediately following the attainment—for me and probably for anyone—are largely about integrating the experience, and harmonizing it with one's inner and outer world. In many ways, this defines the process through the grades above Adeptus Minor—building your life to be a vessel for the True Will that takes it from the internal to the external. Part of my caution and hesitance was to do with this intimacy and specificity. Would this information mean anything to anyone but me? What *could* it mean? Was it even worth talking about it to anyone else? The other part was . . . well . . . it's a dicey endeavor to go out in public and talk about this supposedly "great attainment." It takes a certain tenured standing (or is that a euphemism for my advancing age?) in the eyes of the magical community to be in a place where anyone might actually want to hear about one's personal experiences. In the nearly two decades since my initial experience of K&C, I have come to be in more of such a position in the Thelemic world. Yet, that doesn't mean that my story should in any way front-load or define anyone *else's* experience. Nothing I say in this chapter should be taken to be definitive. Your own eventual experience may be nothing at all like mine.

One reason I have been feeling an increasing interest in discussing my experience, though, is that there's simply not a lot of discussion out there in public view. Few have shared their experiences or results with much transparency or detail. Thus, it can be hard to know what results or consequences you might expect, or even to understand the rough parameters of what *might* happen.

I'm no more special than anyone else—I've just chosen to share my story. The most important and impressive thing to me is that we even *have* structured systems of training that can reliably bring people to the threshold of this attainment. I'm speaking primarily of A∴A∴ and Temple of the Silver Star here, but there are many other orders and more or less formal approaches that accomplish the same thing, even if they would never present themselves as Thelemic, or even locate themselves in the broader Western ceremonial tradition. It's also interesting to note that my understanding of what K&C is, and what it means, has been constantly evolving for the past two decades. This is how it should be, of course—our understanding of our own spiritual attainment can be expected to continue to grow and evolve in depth, range, and detail, as with everything else in our lives.

Before I dive into my own story, I'd like to review some historical views on the HGA, as they have appeared in published works and private letters of early Thelemic luminaries. You will likely also find it useful to review my own general comments on the matter throughout *Living Thelema*.[63]

From "One Star in Sight":

> *It is impossible to lay down precise rules by which a man may attain to the knowledge and conversation of His Holy Guardian Angel; for that is the particular secret of each one of us; a secret not to be told or even divined by any other, whatever his grade. It is the Holy of Holies, whereof each man is his own High Priest, and none knoweth the Name of his brother's God, or the Rite that invokes Him.*[64]

From *Magick in Theory and Practice*:

> *The Single Supreme Ritual is the attainment of the Knowledge and Conversation of the Holy Guardian Angel.* It is the raising of the complete man in a vertical straight line.
>
> **Any deviation from this line tends to become black magic. Any other operation is black magic.** . . . *If the magician needs to perform any other operation than this, it is only lawful in so far as it is a necessary preliminary to That One Work.*[65]

This particular quote communicates a guiding principle that has been central to many of my writings and talks about the subject: All of the tools of the system are *only* there as preliminaries to the K&C working. To be distracted by the tools—to confuse the means with the ends—is a grave (and unfortunately, very common) error.

---

[63] Shoemaker, D. (2022). *Living Thelema: A Practical Guide to Attainment in Aleister Crowley's System of Magick.* Newburyport, MA: Weiser Books.

[64] Crowley, A. (1997). *Magick: Liber ABA* (2nd rev. ed.). Hymenaeus Beta (Ed.). York Beach, ME: Red Wheel/Weiser, LLC, 494.

[65] Ibid., 275.

From the scholion of *Liber Samekh*:

This then is the true aim of the Adept in this whole operation,
to assimilate himself to his Angel by continual conscious com-
munion. For his Angel is an intelligible image of his own true
Will, to do which is the whole of the law of his Being.

Also the Angel appeareth in Tiphereth, which is the heart of
the ruach, and thus the Centre of Gravity of the Mind. It is
also directly inspired from Kether, the Ultimate Self, through
the Path of "The High Priestess," or initiated intuition. Hence
the Angel is in truth the logos or articulate expression of the
whole Being of the Adept, so that as he increases in the perfect
understanding of His name, he approaches the solution of the
ultimate problem: Who he himself truly is.[66]

From *Magick Without Tears*:

[The HGA] is something more than a man, possibly a being
who has already passed through the stage of humanity, and
his peculiarly intimate relationship with his client is that of
friendship, of community, of brotherhood, or Fatherhood. He
is not, let me say with emphasis, a mere abstraction from your-
self; and that is why I have insisted rather heavily that the
term "Higher Self" implies "a damnable heresy and a danger-
ous delusion.[67]

From a letter from Karl Germer to Phyllis Seckler, May 5, 1952:

Keep affirming in your heart your longing, your devotion, to
6S, or the HGA: He is constantly around you, once He has

---

[66] Ibid., 540.

[67] Crowley, A. (1991). *Magick Without Tears*. I. Regardie (Ed.). Scottsdale, AZ: New Falcon, 281–2.

> *found ingress to your soul. He is watching over you, and the*
> *more you begin to perceive His signs, that He is giving you, the*
> *more subtle will become your senses, and get attuned to His*
> *language.*
>
> *Even the apparent difficulties in your life are part of His plan.*
> *One thing that all of us forget is that the clock on higher planes*
> *does not go by hours, days, months and years: the periods are*
> *different; the crime is impatience. The moment you stop desir-*
> *ing, in comes 65. Easy to say, huh? It is the simple things that*
> *are hard!*
>
> *Moreover, it is the HGA Himself who will set the proper day*
> *and hour for the union. Then all will be prepared beautifully*
> *and fall in its place. The leisure, the aspiration, the Yoga, the*
> *surrounding, the silence, and all the rest. Did I not tell you*
> *that He arranged everything for me in the solitude of the Con-*
> *centration Camp? Learn to abandon yourself with utter confi-*
> *dence to Him. Yet, as it is said: Invoke often! Learn the whole*
> *of [Liber] LXV by heart.*[68]

These quotes demonstrate the varying ways Crowley and others have conceived of the HGA across the years. Not only do the views of individuals vary, but they vary within the same individual over time, and it often appears that Crowley emphasized certain aspects of the HGA experience depending on his audience, or the point he was attempting to make at the time. The good news in all of this, as I've said many times, is that *you don't have to know what the HGA is in advance!* If you work the system diligently, gradually building and refining the inner tools that will make the ultimate attainment possible, you'll know everything you need to know when the time comes. Your own experience will answer such questions.

---

[68] Seckler, P. (2017). *The Thoth Tarot, Astrology, & Other Selected Writings.* D. Shoemaker, G. Peters, & R. Johnson (Eds.). Sacramento: Temple of the Silver Star, 297.

Another important thing conveyed in these quotes, and certainly in my experience, is that the HGA is *always* attempting to convey its message to us, via whatever perceptual apparatus is available and efficient. At first, as aspirants working toward K&C, we "hear" the HGA via the medium of our own subconscious, and our own symbol set. Then, when the path of Gimel opens at full K&C, the aspirant's mind in the world of Yetzirah gains *conscious and reliable* access to communications from the HGA, via the world of Briah.

The timing of this attainment is not merely of your own choosing. You can lay out the groundwork for it, of course, making important decisions about timing and circumstances based on your own readiness. Yet, paraphrasing the Holy Books, awaiting is the end, not the beginning. We await the ripeness of the soul to receive the ultimate influx of the Angel's instruction.

Our adventure toward K&C employs every tool available to us. Our personal biography, our lived experience, the parents we had, the culture in which we were raised, the time and circumstances of our incarnation— all of these become potential tools for learning, and for deepening our relationship to the HGA. They *will* be used. Everything you think of as yourself has been there to enable you to be a better talisman of your HGA—an attractor and vessel for the indwelling force of the HGA. You should consider the richness of your experience, your symbolic life, and all the factors above as the *form* that attracts that force.

Our cultural and religious symbols, myths, and subjective experiences will be some of the many influences on our eventual approach to the HGA, and the particular tools that serve us well in that work. We can see how this functioned in Crowley's life, for example. His staunch Christian upbringing instilled a deep relationship with Bible stories, and figures such as the Great Beast and Babalon. Obviously, his particular path of Will was to overturn Old Aeon interpretations of these things, not to simply utilize them as presented by his Plymouth Brethren community. Yet, if he had not had this particular upbringing, he would not likely have been able to transmute these previously fearsome and oppressive symbols into arcana of Light, Life, Love, and Liberty. Wherever we've been, whoever we are, can be utilized by the HGA.

One of the great virtues of the system Crowley left us is that its practicality and pragmatism are keys. Doctrines or dogmas that are conventionally implied by practices from a certain tradition are *not* necessarily implied when we utilize those practices in Thelemic work. An A∴A∴ initiate using a yogic practice might have no inclination whatsoever toward a Hindu belief structure. And so on. So we are left with a toolbox of practices we can use synthetically and syncretically, if and as they work well for us. Furthermore, each individual will bring their own unique strengths to their work. A weakness in any particular branch of practice, such as visualization, ritual work, or meditation, will not generally be an insurmountable obstacle to attainment for the dedicated aspirant, simply because there are so many different practices to draw from. In addition, our training systems intentionally force us to work on areas of weakness rather than allowing us to pander to our strengths, which would make us unbalanced.

Crowley and Germer, as seen in the quotes above, both implied a gendered perception of the HGA: e.g., "when He sets the time" and similar statements. There are a lot of preconceived notions about having an HGA of the opposite gender from one's own identified gender. I have to say, however, that I haven't noticed any such pattern in the reported experiences of students and colleagues over the years. If any gender is perceived at all in the HGA, there does not seem to be a leaning toward either opposite or same-gender manifestations. So, don't get locked into those sorts of expectations.

In some of my earliest talks on the HGA, in my enthusiasm to encourage aspirants about the possibility of their own attainment, I probably didn't balance this encouragement with a corresponding emphasis on skepticism. So I fear what has sometimes happened is that I've made statements about how the HGA "is whispering to you all the time and you just have to listen the right way" and similar conceptions, and aspirants have too easily attributed an impulse, an intuition, or even a genuine flash of illumination to the HGA, immediately and without skepticism. This has sometimes had the very unfortunate side effect of making people decide prematurely that they've "arrived," so they stop seeking and yearning for deeper contact. Accordingly, if you *think* you have had some sort of contact with your HGA: Don't assume it means anything. Don't assume it means nothing. Keep working. Take good notes. Watch for patterns. If something is important enough that you really need to know it, it will be persistent in its efforts to get your attention. There is never going to be a downside to being skeptical, testing any entity that you come across, and questioning and doubting. The reality is there. It's not going anywhere, and the essential messages *will* come through eventually if they are truly important.

Another helpful fact is that if you are working within a structured system like A∴A∴ or TOTSS, you will have landmarks of testing and training that ensure that your blind spots are reduced, that you are not missing important things, that you've looked under all the rocks and corrected personal imbalances, or at least not pandered exclusively to your own preferences and strengths. Then, by the time you get to the point of being ready for the formal K&C working as an Adeptus Minor or the equivalent, you can be reasonably sure that you haven't missed anything crucial, and that the "data" you've received has a greater likelihood of being dependable. You don't *have* to have a teacher or be part of a formal tradition to attain K&C, but it can certainly help for a lot of people. Without these supportive structures, there is increased danger of wasting time due to attempting to "reinvent the wheel," or of failing to explore lesser known and (especially) less desirable aspects of oneself. *All that you are* is useful for this work, so failing to explore yourself fully is like refusing to read the manual before operating a complex piece of machinery. Don't be surprised when it doesn't function correctly or fully!

When it comes to getting ahead of oneself and not assuming too much, I speak from a place of personal experience. When I was a Neophyte working directly under the supervision of Soror Meral, I was practicing with *Liber Samekh* as a part of that curriculum. I had an experience that was very intense, and a Name was communicated to me that I thought might be the Name of my HGA. Over time, I have come to believe this was the experience called the "Vision of the HGA" often assumed to occur at the Neophyte level. I took this information to my teacher, and she conferred the Adeptus Minor 5=6 grade on me, essentially confirming (in her view), "Yes—you've had K&C." While this was flattering, overwhelming, and frankly ego-feeding, it was ultimately something that I couldn't accept. I couldn't simply assume it was true, no matter how much I valued and respected her opinion. So, over the ensuing years, I continued with all the required tasks and tests of the grades of A.·.A.·. beyond Neophyte.

Soror Meral was very understanding of my insistence on this, as she had done the same thing. Karl Germer had recognized her as an Adeptus Minor 5=6 in the 1950s based on her experiences while working as a Probationer, but she subsequently took herself through all the intervening grade tasks just to be sure she'd covered all the bases. This had echoes in Germer's own experience as well—Crowley recognized Germer as a Magister Templi 8=3 of A.·.A.·., even though Germer had certainly not completed the corresponding *formal* grade tasks at that time.

Had I not insisted on passing through the intervening grades and tasks, fully and formally—if I had rested on the conferral of grades that had been handed to me—I would have missed a *universe* of experience. In retrospect, I cannot imagine how the rest of my life would have proceeded from there, under those circumstances. It is *so* important to check the boxes of testing and training, to the extent that we can, in whatever system (or lack of system) we are operating within. Be very careful not to short-circuit yourself by assuming you've arrived, when you *might* merely have just begun the journey. Let's say you've actually attained K&C, but you continue to walk through the grade tasks. In this situation, the *worst-case* scenario is that you deepen your connection to the HGA by doing so, and it takes a little longer. That's certainly not a waste of time! The *best-case* scenario is that you avoid the horror of having shortchanged yourself an absolute cornerstone of self-discovery and empowerment in True Will.

Many people will get a *possibly* authentic Name early in their process, as I did. However, just because it's common doesn't mean it always happens, or that it even *needs* to happen for any given aspirant. Some people don't get the Name until they're in the midst of their K&C working. I've never known anyone to have K&C who did not *eventually* receive a Name, however. It is often useful to think of the HGA's Name as a "formula" of your True Will. The *lived* True Will in your life is the voice of the HGA whispering to you. The process of getting a Name, and understanding it as a formula of your True Will and the nature of your HGA, occurs in human consciousness at the Yetziratic and Briatic level. It's still consciousness *about* something that is trans-egoic and trans-Abyssal. In other words, the Name is a translation into human consciousness of something which is itself ineffable and inexpressible.

The way I think of it, the HGA "lives" in Kether, but you first encounter it with full conscious awareness in Tiphareth. This is your point of contact—the marriage bed where the balanced and awakened human *ruach* is joined with the descending power of the path of Gimel from Kether. The *ruach* is not destroyed; rather, K&C represents the beginnings of a more complete ego-transparency where you can perceive the communications of the HGA much more consciously and directly. And then, like the archetypal Hero returning to their homeland with the gold they have found, you bring this boon from your HGA to the outer world through the intermediary of your *ruach*.

With these preliminaries out of the way, let me describe my actual process with the work, and the circumstances of my life at the time.

In the last years of Soror Meral's life, approximately 2000 to 2004 e.v., I had been working closely with her at her home in Oroville, California. I was living just an hour and a half away in Sacramento, of course. We had become the best of friends, in addition to our official magical relationship, and I was clearly being groomed as her primary administrative successor—she'd had a serious falling out with one senior student around 2000, and another senior student was drawn to more independent work. As early 2004 rolled around, she was preparing to die soon—predicting it down to the day, in fact. She had transferred her library and archives to me at my home in Sacramento as a part of her preparations to move out of her beloved home, and into assisted living. On the last day of May 2004, I was traveling to see my father, who was himself dying of cancer. The necessity of this visit to my father was the *only* reason I wasn't by Phyllis's side at the time of her death, and I got the call informing me of her passing while in an airport on this journey. Thus, my dying father was the reason I couldn't be with my dying friend and teacher. My marriage also happened to be dying. (Detecting a theme here?) I was wrestling intensely with the heartache of seeing the marriage end, and knowing the effects it would likely have on our son, who was only eight years old at the time.

So, all of this is to say that as I finished up my Dominus Liminis grade work and stared down the barrel of what my mundane life was bringing to me, a hell of a lot of true magick was happening. I knew it was time. I just knew. It was "time" for the working based on the A∴A∴ grade I was working on, but it was also the right *kairos*—a rightness of *sacred time* rather than chronological time.[69] I was on a plane reading Gopi Krishna's book *Kundalini,*[70] but I found that each time I read about his experiences with spontaneous *kundalini* activity in his own life, I would feel those "zaps" myself. It was literally impossible for me to continue to read the material at that moment. I was just "too ready" for the next step in the Great Work, or it ready for me, and I felt compelled to make formal arrangements to pursue the retirement and the final working in December.

---

[69] For more on the concept of *kairos*, see Shoemaker, D. (2016). *The Winds of Wisdom: Visions from the Thirty Enochian Aethyrs.* Sacramento: Anima Solis Books.

[70] Krishna, G. (1997). *Kundalini: The Evolutionary Energy in Man* (rev. ed.). Boulder, CO: Shambhala Publications.

In the midst of knowing my father was dying and my marriage was ending, and not knowing what the hell I was going to do about either of these situations, I came up with an interesting plan: "I'll just do this retirement, and the guy who comes out on the other side can figure it all out! He'll be an Adept, after all, and surely so much wiser than I am." That was the best I could manage, in my feeble ego state. Sometimes that's all we can do—surrender to our deeper Truth. It was as if the universe said: "Let's strip away everything you might identify with. I dare you to discover the core of what's left. Let's strip away the things that tempt you to attach to them, and in that rawness, nakedness, and vulnerability, you'll find the real seed of yourself—the *khabs*-star at the core of your *khu*-veil—in a deeper and fuller way than ever before."

It seems apparent to me that the intensity of this "stripping away" will tend to correspond to our existing level of unhelpful attachment to these aspects of our identity. These may manifest as drives toward safety, certainty, dependency, money, status, and so on, but the specific mix will undoubtedly vary with the individual case. Not everyone will have a difficult time. In my own example, however, I would say that for some reason, I needed to feel some loss, some emptiness; to be confused and searching for next steps; to be *unable* to rest within the safety of my existing life. I had to be ready to toss all of that away.

The further we progress along the path of true inner initiation, the less the universe allows us to stray from the path of True Will. Imagine you are walking down a corridor with elastic walls. Early in the path, if you start to make missteps, you can get quite a way off the correct route before you start to "feel" the pushback—the corridor's walls are more elastic and forgiving. The world around you will *eventually* make the point to you, but it may take a while. Later on, as you advance in awareness of and commitment to True Will, especially after K&C, the feedback seems almost immediate—sometimes so immediate it doesn't even register consciously. In any case, regardless of the timing of this universal feedback mechanism, its intensity will tend to correspond to how "off track" we are from the path of True Will. In my case, I really, truly needed a life overhaul in order to actualize my potential and my Will. I was told so in no uncertain terms by the events unfolding around me, and by the pain I felt inside me. All of this drove me to make important choices that I might not have been prepared to make had I not gone through these hardships.

I decided to do an 11-week retirement based on a hybrid of material in *Liber Samekh* and *Liber VIII*—two important writings of Crowley's on the potential structure and process of the K&C working. The program I devised had a gradually intensifying pace of working, i.e. one week of *Samekh* once per day, two weeks at twice per day, and so on, all culminating in a final week of complete solitary retirement. This was pre-smartphones and such, so it was easier then, but it wouldn't have mattered. I'd had more than enough of the outer world for a while!

The location of the working was the newly built Soror Meral Building in Sacramento, a purpose-built Thelemic temple I had helped design, in the back of a home that I would later co-own. Soror Meral had lived long enough to see the blueprints, but sadly not quite long enough to see the completed structure. The local Thelemic community had assisted with construction at various points. One memorable occasion was when 8 or 10 of us erected the walls, like some sort of modern Thelemic equivalent of a traditional barn-raising. My K&C retirement there was the first use of the building.

This building itself was quite a "battery" of magical force. In the walls, ceiling, and floor were the Trumps of the Thoth Tarot deck corresponding to the various dimensions of the "Cube of Space." Embedded in the floor, running west to east, were the seven Trumps attributed to the chakras. And perhaps most importantly, a copy of *The Book of the Law* was buried in the foundation at the eastern end of the temple.

An air mattress and a little writing desk were in the east. The shrine and altar I built for the core aspects of the working were in the center—a spot that still gives me ecstatic thrills whenever I stand there. The inner walls of the building weren't even up yet—just insulation covered with sheets, which barely kept out the December cold. My air mattress would gradually deflate after several hours of sleep, waking me via the cold floor's contact with my back. But all of this was *fine*.

I entered the retirement not knowing what would happen, but knowing it was *all I had*. Everything had fallen away except the core of whoever or whatever I was going to turn out to be. In the final week, things really started to roll. Over the past 10 weeks, I had continued to see therapy clients and spend time with my family—most importantly, my son—and had managed to work the increasingly frequent invocations into a relatively normal pace of life. This meant that sometimes—on a long drive to a vacation spot, for example—I'd simply have to let my wife know it was "time for me to do my thing," and I'd close my eyes, go silent, and do the entire *Liber Samekh* ritual in my astral body while she drove. And that's what you have to do, when you're not independently wealthy, and therefore unable to spend the full 11 weeks away from the rest of humanity.

This led to the final week of solitary retirement, which was (as I had hoped) where things would really take off. I went in with my usual habits of daily ritual and diary keeping. It's worth noting that I don't typically write very much, in my diary or even generally. A long diary entry, for me, might be one full page. Yet immediately on entering the retirement, I started getting what felt like "downloads" of 10–15 pages of material *per day* coming through. And the character of the material was unlike anything that I could have come up with in my conscious mind. It was qualitatively and quantitatively beyond anything I had ever contemplated. It felt entirely like it was *presented* to me, not "thought of" *by* me. And at this point, I had the first glimmers of just how much I would have missed if, as described above, I had simply accepted Phyllis's conferral of 5=6 some six years earlier! Quite simply, I didn't know what I didn't know!

So, at the climax, in the center of the shrine, the working was concluded around Winter Solstice 2004. What was it like? First of all, a strong sense of presence. If you can imagine the strongest sense of someone *being with you* that you've ever experienced, and multiply it many times over . . . it was more than that. Like I was, inside and out, within a cocoon of intense but completely equilibrated warmth, truth, and love. There is Light of a peculiar quality, almost like the air is filled with a mist that isn't mist. Not visible yet not invisible either. There is a thickness and intensity in the atmosphere—like the "space between the molecules" is somehow alive. I cheekily dubbed it "holy smoke" in my diary. But all of this is a mere attempt to slap words onto a subjective experience that perhaps can't ever be described fully.

In the aftermath of the working—days, weeks, months, eventually years—I attempted to integrate all that had occurred. I have an ever-evolving (and lengthening!) document that contains all the data from the original retirement, but also my ongoing reflections since that time. It is a record of my attempts to deepen my understanding of the material, but also to implement it in my personal life, and (ultimately, as it happened) into the magical orders I administer. I'm sure this will continue for the rest of my life. This is always the task of the new Adept—to build their outer lives into a vessel for what they have learned, to attempt to equilibrate the inner and outer worlds based on the new realities that have been glimpsed.

In practical terms, this meant finalizing the end of my marriage and moving on with my personal life. It meant grieving the loss of my father and my teacher, and trusting that in my HGA I had the only teacher I still required. And soon after, in 2008, it meant founding the Temple of the Silver Star as a training vehicle for the material I had essentially been commanded by my HGA to codify. I began the *Living Thelema* podcast, and the writings that eventually became the associated book. Everything that any of you likely know about me has happened *since my K&C attainment.*

If everything leading up to K&C is a courtship, and the K&C itself is a wedding, then what comes after is, like any marriage, something you have to work at! Sometimes I feel closer to the HGA, sometimes I feel further away—and the *feel* of the relationship has evolved over the years. I have never stopped feeling the *presence* and guidance of the HGA, despite fluctuations in the level of intensity; instead, it has been a question of the *way* this ongoing guidance is experienced. What happened, writ large, is that it went from a clear sense of there being "an external entity telling me things" to a much more internalized and nuanced state, almost like the HGA has become a deep voice of conscience so integrated into *who I am* that it doesn't feel external anymore. Germer references this same phenomenon in some of his letters to Phyllis and to Jane Wolfe.

A lot of things in your life may change after K&C—relationships, careers, and so on—though this isn't always the case. Regardless, one of the seemingly invariable characteristics is that what you are taught by the HGA will simultaneously be so far beyond anything you thought of as *yourself*, and also explain everything you've ever been. It's that sort of a paradox. The thought, "Wow, I had no idea this was even possible!" coexists with "Oh! Now it totally makes sense why my life experiences, my psychological makeup, and my personal skill set are what they are," and "All those shitty things that happened to me turned out to shape me in *exactly* the way I needed to bring me to this place." If nothing else, on a psychological and emotional level, I would encourage you to take heart in those times when it seems like the universe is shitting on you in the worst way, and to trust that if you stick with it, you'll discover why. I hate to sound like I'm parroting the Christian "God has a plan for you" trope, but if you can have hope that you will *eventually* find utility, and a refining fire, in your ordeals, you'll be on the right track.

∴

The following are some questions that have been presented to me during various lectures on this topic. I find that engaging in Q&A with seekers is one of the most effective ways of clarifying my own understanding, so I am presenting my responses (often verbatim) in the hope that they might shed more light.

What are the landmarks that can help us verify we're on the "right track"?

As noted previously, one very concrete landmark is your grade in A∴A∴, TOTSS, or whatever formal system you might be working in (if any).

The system exists to provide a graded set of dependable landmarks. If you "buy" that the system is effective, and you've been working it diligently, under competent supervision, then you deserve to have some confidence that the grades are meaningful statements about your spiritual evolution.

Beyond that, there are signs of feedback from the universe all along the way. Any time you are living and acting in harmony with True Will, you will likely have a fairly intense sense that you are on the right track. Perhaps it will be an awareness that you're really in your element performing a certain activity, or that you feel fully alive doing another. Be aware of the moments when you feel most fully yourself, and in the flow of life; and the times when you feel like something greater than yourself is working *through* you without too much intervention on the part of your conscious self. Perhaps you will feel like doors open to you easily when you make certain choices, or that you are swimming with the current of life instead of against it. These are all likely vibrant signs of True Will in action and, by definition, evidence that you are correctly heeding the direction of your HGA. Joy and rapture, things of beauty, are all glimmers of the Angel's presence and influence.

Do one's interests and proclivities in magical technology point at the means by which one might build a ritual structure to attain K&C?

On my path toward K&C, especially once I entered final stages of the 11-week working, all kinds of tools were presented to me. I was given magical signs and postures to use, words or phrases intended to make it easier to "get back" to the HGA for the next day's work, and much more. I was building my own personal religion, as its High Priest and Prophet. The regalia, liturgy, devotional practices, and everything else about it were gradually devised as an intimate collaboration between me and my HGA. All the various magical interests I'd ever had were put to use, in one way or another. All my strengths were utilized, and my weaknesses somehow compensated for. Everything about me that *worked well* was tapped by the HGA for use.

Does one's relationship with the HGA supersede one's relationship with deity or spirit?

I would be inclined to use those terms synonymously with "HGA" in this context. As you are approaching K&C, there is in my view no better way of understanding what the HGA is than pure spirit, directed in a straight line toward you alone. So, that's your access point. Your relationship to spirit *is* your relationship to the HGA. Any previous work with other deities will likely immediately feel partial by comparison—an approximation, or a profile view, as if you had previously had a grip on only the left arm of the HGA, and now you're embracing the whole thing.

Can you say more about "invoking often" and "enflaming oneself in prayer"?

Any excuse you have for practicing the muscles of invocation will help you in your path toward K&C. This is something available to you every day if you're doing *Liber Resh*, for example. Four times a day, you have a chance to invoke an aspect of deity, and during the "Unity" section, you have a chance to invoke the oneness behind all these partial aspects. If you like, the quarterly adorations, much like *Liber Astarte*, allow you to worship an intentionally partial aspect of deity with all your might; but then, in the Unity section, you adore the idea of the undivided unity beyond all things, symbolized by the Sun. For those in the pre-K&C phase of aspiration, anything we can conceptualize as the "ultimate deity," "highest divinity," "godhead," and so on is our closest approximation to the eventual reality of the HGA. That's simply the best our *ruach* can do prior to K&C. Our everyday minds are limited to the creation of "masks" of divinity, and we cannot consciously behold divinity itself, as we can after K&C. "Invoking often" gives us practice with those muscles we will eventually need to use in a very directed and specific way with the HGA.

Inflaming oneself in prayer involves a related set of devotional tools for firing up our ecstasy—also essential muscles for the greater work of K&C. In everyday practice, you can practice this by focusing on the awesome power and magnitude of the Archangels of the Lesser Ritual of the Pentagram, or the Kether-point in its Qabalistic Cross section. And again, as noted above, striving to conceive of the all-powerful unity at the conclusion of the *Liber Resh* adoration is a great way of stoking the flames. These are just a few examples; any time you can dive deeper into devotion during a ritual or practice, it will help. *Fall in love* with the entities you are interacting with, and even with the *idea* of such entities. When you have trained yourself to make a *concept* as sexy as hell, and that in turn fires up your religious devotion, you're on the right track—but this takes a good bit of practice. All of this will be helped immeasurably as you monitor your own progress, of course. Your experience will be your best teacher with regard to what works for you.

In the early stages of the path, how important is it to have some conception of the form of the HGA, vs. opting for fluidity or absence of form? "White light" vs. towering humanoid forms, etc.

Anything we can imagine at the aspirant stage is just a mask or veil over the underlying reality of the HGA, and we must keep that in mind. I would caution you not to front-load your work with preconceptions about what you should be seeing, hearing, feeling, or otherwise experiencing. Following your own path of breadcrumbs, learning your own HGA's language, is the key. It may be largely visual, but it may be something entirely different; and of course the forms that ultimately appear will not necessarily remind you of any existing religious iconography. I often think that Ra-Hoor-Khuit serves as a convenient "stand-in" for our own HGA. It helps to have a vibrant god-form to latch onto as we aspire, especially since that particular deity is of such central importance to the New Aeon; but that absolutely does not mean your own HGA will necessarily resemble Ra-Hoor-Khuit physically, or in terms of its character or other attributes. That said, you may find useful clues in which images seem to fire you up, since they may help you understand key ingredients in your own formulae of aspiration.

All that said, I think the most important thing of all is that compared to other interactions you may have had with any other sort of spirit, archangel, etc., the experience of K&C is on an entirely different level of intensity and specificity. It's like the difference between a conversation with a stranger on the bus and the most intense sex of your life. You won't mistake it for anything else! Yet it is not the "spiritual orgasm" alone that makes the experience—it is the specificity of that experience with regard to your own nature and path, and the *fruits* of that experience in your subsequent conscious living.[71] It's not difficult to whip up ample "energized enthusiasm" via intense ritual, breathwork, drugs, music, or ecstatic dance; but the goal with K&C is to *target* all that enthusiasm toward the HGA with single-minded devotion, unerring aim, an entirely focused mind, and complete receptivity to the HGA's eventual embrace.

∴

It is my hope that these words are somehow inspiring to you as you find your own way on the path. Believe in yourself, and persist. If you're moving *at all*, you're not stuck, so don't fall prey to insecurities that try to tell you aren't progressing—it's very likely that your progress won't be clearly discernible, definable, or otherwise tangible until you've moved just a bit past each individual step. Trust that you will find the tools, the clues, and the assistance you truly need.

---

[71] I strongly recommend that you review Crowley's scholion on *Liber Samekh* (especially Point III) in light of all these comments. It is quite simply one of the most important instructional texts Crowley ever wrote, and should, in my opinion, be the subject of constant study for all aspirants.

SUN OF BEING (1991)[72]

Let us open our hearts and minds to the Highest
And throw off the veil of negative existence.
Come, let us tread among the stars of the blessed
Let us control the evidence of happenstance.

Let us see the world as pure phenomena of Will
Formed by ourselves in our going.
Let us see Adonai's hand in everything, but still
A making by ourselves, our seeds sowing.

Upon the bosom of earth our deeds are awaiting
The flowering of earth's bounty in roots and seeds
In leaves, flowers and fruits in true trysting with experience,
A wholesome result of our deeds.

Whatever we do, there is no escape from growth,
There is no escape from nature's way.
The Law is that the soul must come forth
From delusion and terror to seek the light of day.

The sun is our nurturance, our aim, our goal
Center of being, each one's life essence;

[72] Seckler, P. (2017). *Collected Poems 1946–1996*. D. Shoemaker & L. Gardner (Eds.). Sacramento: Temple of the Silver Star, 106–7.

The sun is nature's law, of bounties untold;
The sun is in our hearts, a shield and defense.

The sun is our nature's pure being, a sensation
Reflected and absorbed in earth nature's breast.
We are that sun of being, that absorption
In the all, we are each a star in this feast.

Between sun and earth, own this grounding, this
     territory seen
As growth, our exploration of ourselves as a Hadit
The point of light nestled in the bosom of phenomena
An outcome of our wedding with and love for Nuit.

—PHYLLIS SECKLER (Soror Meral)

INDEX

ABOUT THE AUTHOR

Dr. David Shoemaker is a clinical psychologist in private practice, specializing in Jungian and cognitive-behavioral psychotherapy. David is the Chancellor and Prolocutor of the Temple of the Silver Star (*totss.org*). He is a long-standing member of Ordo Templi Orientis (*oto.org*) and A∴A∴ (*onestarinsight.org*), and has many years of experience training initiates in these traditions.

He is a Past Master of 418 Lodge of O.T.O. (now 418 Oasis) in Sacramento, having succeeded Soror Meral (Phyllis Seckler), his friend and teacher. He also serves as a Sovereign Grand Inspector General of the order. David was the founding President of the O.T.O. Psychology Guild, and he is a frequent speaker at national and regional events. A consecrated Bishop of Ecclesia Gnostica Catholica, David led the team that developed the Pastoral Counseling Workshops and brought them to O.T.O. members across the U.S.

David was a co-editor of the journals *Neshamah* (Psychology Guild) and *Cheth* (418 Lodge). In addition to his essays in these publications, his writings have been published in the journals *Mezlim* and *Black Pearl*, and his chapter on Qabalistic psychology was included in the Instructor's Manual of Fadiman and Frager's *Personality and Personal Growth*, an undergraduate psychology textbook. He was the compiler of *Jane Wolfe: The Cefalu Diaries 1920–1923* and a co-editor of the collections of the writings of Phyllis Seckler: *The Thoth Tarot, Astrology, & Other Selected Writings*, and *The Kabbalah, Magick, and Thelema, Selected Writings Vol. II*. His popular *Living Thelema* instructional segments are presented regularly on the podcast of the same name, and the influential book of the same title was published in 2013. David's record of scrying the thirty Enochian Aethyrs, *The Winds of Wisdom*, was published in late 2016, and his most recent work is *Llewellyn's Complete Book of Ceremonial Magick*, co-edited with Lon Milo DuQuette.

In addition to his work in magick and psychology, David is a composer and musician. He lives in North Carolina.

LIVINGTHELEMA.COM

Temple of the Silver Star—Academic Track

The Temple of the Silver Star is a non-profit religious and educational corporation, based on the principles of Thelema. It was founded in service to the A∴A∴, under warrant from Soror Meral (Phyllis Seckler), to provide preparatory training in magick, mysticism, Qabalah, Tarot, astrology, and much more. In its academic track, each student is assigned an individual teacher, who provides one-to-one instruction and group classes. Online classes and other distance learning options are available.

Temple of the Silver Star—Initiatory Track

The Temple of the Silver Star's initiatory track offers ceremonial initiation, personalized instruction, and a complete system of training in the Thelemic Mysteries. Our degree system is based on the Qabalistic Tree of Life and the cipher formulæ of the Golden Dawn, of which we are a lineal descendant.

Our entire curriculum is constructed to be in conformity with the Law of Thelema, and our central aim is to guide each aspirant toward the realization of their purpose in life, or True Will. In order to empower our members to discover and carry out their True Will, we teach Qabalah, Tarot, ceremonial magick, meditation, astrology, and much more. Our initiates meet privately for group ceremonial and healing work, classes, and other instruction. We occasionally offer public classes and rituals.

Active participation in a local Temple or Pronaos is the best way to maximize the benefits of our system. However, we do offer at-large memberships for those living at some distance from one of our local bodies.

If you are interested in learning more about the work of the Temple of the Silver Star, we invite you to submit an application via our website, or to contact us with questions.

TOTSS.ORG

Do what thou wilt shall be the whole of the Law.

The A∴A∴ is the system of spiritual attainment established by Aleister Crowley and George Cecil Jones in the early 1900s, as a modern expression of the Inner School of wisdom that has existed for millennia. Its central aim is simply to lead each aspirant toward their own individual attainment, for the betterment of all humanity. The course of study includes a diversity of training methods, such as Qabalah, raja yoga, ceremonial magick, and many other traditions. A∴A∴ is not organized into outer social organizations, fraternities, or schools; rather, it is based on the time-tested power of individual teacher–student relationships, under the guidance of the masters of the Inner School. All training and testing is done strictly in accordance with *Liber CLXXXV* and other foundational documents.

Those interested in pursuing admission into A∴A∴ are invited to initiate contact via the following addresses:

A∴A∴
P.O. Box 215483
Sacramento, CA 95821
onestarinsight.org

The Student phase of preparation for work in A∴A∴ begins by acquiring a specific set of reference texts, notifying A∴A∴ of the same, and studying the texts for at least three months. The Student may then request Examination. More information about this process is available via the Cancellarius at the addresses given above. NOTE: While our primary mailing address is in California, supervising Neophytes are available in many countries around the world.

If you are called to begin this journey, we earnestly invite you to contact us. Regardless of your choice in this matter, we wish you the best as you pursue your own Great Work. May you attain your True Will!

Love is the law, love under will.

ORDO TEMPLI ORIENTIS
AND ECCLESIA
GNOSTICA CATHOLICA

Those interested in learning more about O.T.O. and E.G.C. may initiate contact via the following websites:

In the United States:

oto-usa.org

In other countries:

oto.org

OTHER WORKS BY DAVID SHOEMAKER

As author:

Living Thelema (book and podcast)

The Winds of Wisdom: Visions from the Thirty Enochian Aethyrs

Various essays and rituals, published in the journals *Mezlim, Agape, Black Pearl, Neshamah*, and *Cheth*

As editor or co-editor:

Jane Wolfe: The Cefalu Diaries 1920–1923

Karl Germer: Selected Letters 1928–1962

Llewellyn's Complete Book of Ceremonial Magick

Phyllis Seckler (Soror Meral): The Thoth Tarot, Astrology, & Other Selected Writings

Phyllis Seckler (Soror Meral): The Kabbalah, Magick, and Thelema, Selected Writings Vol. II

Phyllis Seckler (Soror Meral): Collected Poems 1946–1996

As musician and composer:

Elsa Letterseed (feature film score)

Last Three Lives (self-titled)

Last Three Lives: Via

Workings (2000–2010)

As organizer:

ThelemaCon (biennial public Thelemic conference) *thelemacon.org*

TO OUR READERS

Weiser Books, an imprint of Red Wheel/Weiser, publishes books across the entire spectrum of occult, esoteric, speculative, and New Age subjects. Our mission is to publish quality books that will make a difference in people's lives without advocating any one particular path or field of study. We value the integrity, originality, and depth of knowledge of our authors.

Our readers are our most important resource, and we appreciate your input, suggestions, and ideas about what you would like to see published.

Visit our website at *www.redwheelweiser.com*, where you can learn about our upcoming books and free downloads, and also find links to sign up for our newsletter and exclusive offers.

You can also contact us at *info@rwwbooks.com* or at

Red Wheel/Weiser, LLC
65 Parker Street, Suite 7
Newburyport, MA 01950